Seeing

Christ

IN THE
Old Testament
(The Jewish Scriptures)

Ervin N. Hershberger

Distributed by
CHOICE BOOKS OF NORTHERN VIRGINIA
11923 Lee Highway, Fairfax, VA 22030
(703)830-2800
We Welcome Your Response

Printed by Campbell Copy Center
Harrisonburg, Virginia

ISBN: 0-940883-10-4

1st Edition Printing 1999
Expanded Edition Printing 2000

TABLE OF CONTENTS

DEDICATION

I heartily dedicate this book to Jesus Christ,
our SAVIOR, LORD, and MASTER.
He is the Heart and Fiber of the whole Bible.
Without Him even the Book of books could
not offer a message of salvation.

CREDITS DUE

To God the Father who gives to all men life and breath.
To Jesus Christ who died that I may live in and for Him.
To the Holy Spirit who motivates and enables for service.

To my faithful wife Barbara for helping to double-check references, and for standing with me these fifty-nine years, understanding, undergirding and encouraging me as only a dedicated companion would or could.

To Marvin Yoder, Mildred Yoder, and Kenton Yoder (Son-in-law, Daughter, and Grandson) for editing my manuscripts and giving many helpful suggestions.

To Simon Schrock, Fairfax, VA, and others for their encouragement, prayer support, and blessings.

To Lonnie Yoder, Harrisonburg, VA, and everyone else who helped to design a meaningful cover.

To Craig Wenger, Harrisonburg, VA, for setting the type.

To Campbell Copy Center, Harrisonburg, VA for their final touch and printing the book.

May Christ be glorified by revealing Himself to us on page after page in the Sacred Book of the Ages!

INTRODUCTION

Do you remember those favorite Bible stories from the Old Testament that have been told thousands of times and concluded with a brief "moral of the story"? These stories are still being told. However, the Old Testament is often viewed as a book of interesting stories from another era with a moral lesson to be learned. While this may be true, it is much more.

Seeing Christ in the Old Testament reveals that an illuminating thread of Jesus Christ is woven throughout the fabric of the entire Old Testament. The author saw sixty nine reminders of Jesus flash across the "Inspired Screen" in the first thirty one verses of the Bible. He saw Jesus show up on page after page of the inspired Word of God.

The Lord Jesus Christ is very present in the creation story. He is included in every Hebrew name of God. There are types and shadows of Him in the characters of those "favorite stories" of the Old Testament. "Christ shows up" where we haven't thought of looking for Him.

How could the colorful life of Moses foreshadow the ministry of Christ? Or the reign of Solomon be typical of Christ at His second coming? How could Christ be seen in the fascinating account of iron rising from the bottom of the Jordan River? How could a shadow of Christ be in the master piercing the ear of his servant? A type of Christ can be seen throughout the Old Testament, beginning with Adam and flowing on through to the prophets. It is an enlightening experience to see Christ typified in the familiar accounts of Noah, Abraham, Joseph, Samuel, David, Elijah, and many others.

Seeing Christ in the Old Testament puts additional light and life into those "favorite stories". It affirms the value of reading and making the entire Bible a part of the believers life. It affirms that all scripture is given by the inspiration of God and is profitable for our learning.

The author frequently refers to the German Bible. His ability to read and study in German adds to the richness of insights the Lord has given him. His reference to Greek meaning of words helps give clarity to what sometimes seem to be difficult passages.

This book nurtures an intimate relationship with Jesus Christ. It shows Him exalted to the position of King of kings to whom every tongue shall confess that He is Lord. It has been a joyful experience seeing Jesus Christ appearing again and again in the names and accounts in the Old Testament. It is with joy that I enthusiastically recommend this book.

- Simon Schrock

PREFACE

Christ is man's greatest Treasure. Without Him our Bibles would be skeletons. He is the frame and fabric of the Old Testament as well as of the New. The Law and the Prophets pointed forward, while the Gospels and the Epistles point back to Christ. He is the central focus of both.

The history of fallen man is included for our warning and instruction, to show us how much we need Christ. Knowledge without the Savior would be like dreams without substance, or husks without kernels. People speak of the Old Testament as dry reading, and some even wonder why we have it. It was written to prepare fallen man for the coming Messiah, and to point us to Him.

I have not discussed Old Testament sacrifices or rituals. That is a study of its own, and Bible readers know that they point forward to Christ. I chose to address the Hebrew names for God and the typology of Bible characters, because they have vital meaning for us today.

Types and shadows are like the parables of Jesus. His disciples asked Him why He speaks in parables. He explained that to His disciples it is given to know the mysteries of the kingdom of heaven, but to the *disinterested* it is not given. If you ever feel the shadows are dim, remember the Substance is clear, and the search is rewarding. We find treasures where our heart is.

Part I (Chapters 1 and 2 is a glimpse of Christ in eternity past, "in His glory which He had with the Father before the world was." Christ is the very One by whom God made the worlds. He is the express image of God's person, and upholds all things by the word of His power. (John 17:5, 1:1-3,10 Hebrews 1:2-3)

Part II (Chapters 3-14) is seeing Christ, in perfect union with the Father in the Hebrew names for God. The names for God are also used for Christ, who was actively involved in the history of God's people for about four thousand years before

9

His virgin birth in Bethlehem. The names of God are full of meaning. They make a fascinating and inspiring study.

This study is limited because I cannot read Hebrew nor Greek, and finite minds cannot fully comprehend **Infinity**. We do have Bible concordances and dictionaries that interpret these names in English, which most of us can read (See bibliography, page 185). Others may use a different spelling for some of these names. I used English letters and tried to follow the spelling used by Strong's Concordance. For example, instead of Yaweh or J^{e}hovah I simply used the English rendering Jehovah. I assumed most of my readers would prefer it that way. Anyone fluent in the in the Hebrew language, may be frustrated by my limitations. I trust Him who spoke through Balaam's donkey, to somehow bless these feeble efforts.

Part III (Chapters 15-28) is seeing various aspects of Christ in the flesh foreshadowed in the many Old Testament Bible characters. Some types are very obvious while others may be debatable. It is my persuasion that God designed to show us Christ in numerous types and shadows, figures of speech, or names and titles where we haven't even thought of looking for Him.

Part IV (Chapters 29-30) is seeing Christ in eternity future committed to serve "for ever," yet reigning in supernal glory as "KING OF KINGS, AND LORD OF LORDS" (Rev. 19:16. He will then have at least one more name not yet revealed to man (Rev. 19:13).

These studies have potential far beyond this writer's ability to capture. The book is neither comprehensive nor exhaustive. I only hope it may whet your appetite for personal study, and intensify your appreciation for Christ. To **Him** be praise and glory!

Part I

Seeing Christ
in
Eternity Past

But thou, Bethlehem..., out of thee shall He come forth unto me that is to be ruler in Israel; whose goings forth have been from of old, from everlasting.
Micah 5:2

1

SEEING CHRIST
IN THE BEGINNING

Glimpses of His pre-incarnate Glory,
which He had with the Father
before the world was. John 17:5

In the beginning **GOD**

Nothing else	— No earth	— No sea
No sky	— No sun	— No moon
No stars	— No people	— Nothing but...

GOD

We bury our faces, and cry

HOLY   HOLY   HOLY!

13

GOD's greatness far transcends the comprehension of the most brilliant human mind! He "humbleth himself to behold the things that are in heaven, and in the earth" (Ps. 113:6). Yet in His infinite love for mankind He stoops down to reveal Himself to us by a multitude of illustrations, types, and shadows, so that we may learn to know Him.

Being one God in three Persons, He created the universe with many triads and trinities. This may be *Primer Lesson Number One* toward understanding God as a Holy Tri-unity. Then, as a climax, He created man a trichotomy of spirit, soul, and body—in the image and as a dim shadow of Himself. Following are a few of the trinities God created for our benefit.

A. The UNIVERSE is a trinity of TIME, SPACE, and MATTER
Each of these fills everything, everywhere, all the time.

B. TIME is a trinity of FUTURE, PRESENT, PAST.
The present always flows out of the future, and moves
on into the past.

C. SPACE has LENGTH, BREADTH, and HEIGHT (OR DEPTH).
All are everywhere all the time—never missing anywhere.

D. MATTER exists as ENERGY, MOTION, PHENOMENA.
All are omnipresent; and motion coming out of energy, produces phenomena (experienced by physical senses)[1]

E. The SUN is LIGHT, HEAT, and ENERGY
There is nothing hid from the heat thereof (Psalm 19:6)

F. MAN consists of SPIRIT, SOUL, and BODY
In the image and likeness of the Holy Trinity (Gen. 1:26)

Even the six creation days are set up in three related pairs: first and fourth; second and fifth; third and sixth. On the first day God created Light; on the fourth day He created lights (sun, moon and stars). On the second day He divided the

---

[1]Nathan R. Wood in *The Trinity in the Universe*. With permission from Kregel Publications.

waters above the firmament from the waters below the firmament (leaving just enough moisture in the air to make a good breathing atmosphere); on the fifth day He made fish to inhabit the waters, and flying fowl to inhabit the atmosphere. On the third day He made dry land, trees and vegetation; on the sixth day He made the creatures and man that inhabit the dry land and eat the vegetation.

The basic moral attribute of God is **holiness**, the theme song of heaven (Isa. 6:3; Rev. 4:8). One of His most endearing attributes is *love*. We all agree that "God is love" (1 John 4:8, 16). Love requires relationship and without plurality there is no relationship. So it is self-evident that even when there was nothing but GOD—before creation began—God was a Plurality, for "God is love." There was the Lover, the Beloved, and the mutual Spirit of Love between the Three.

God is Spirit, and they that worship Him must worship Him in Spirit and in truth. "But the natural man receiveth not the things of the Spirit of God: for they are foolishness unto him: neither can he know them, because they are spiritually discerned" (1 Cor. 2:14). All we really know about God is what He has revealed to us of Himself.

God's power and glory are revealed in what He has created (Ps. 19:1-6). He reveals Himself more fully in His Word, the Bible. We learn little by little, progressively, as we are able to receive it, but it must be spiritually discerned. Finally, He revealed Himself to us most perfectly in Jesus Christ, "the **express image** of his person" (Heb. 1:3). "He that hath seen [Jesus] hath seen the Father" (John 14:9).

By simple, trusting faith and humble obedience we learn more about God than human reasoning could ever teach us. His Word is truth. It is more important for us to believe His Word than it is to fully understand it. To learn about the universe we begin with Him who made it all. He who was and **is the Beginning** of it all, has introduced Himself through the prophet Isaiah:

"Who hath wrought and done it, calling the generations from the **beginning?** I the LORD, the **first,** and with the **last;** I am he" (Isa. 41:4).

"Thus saith the LORD the King of Israel, and his *redeemer* the LORD of hosts; I am the **first,** and I am the last; and beside me there is no God" (Isa. 44:6).

Both verses reveal Christ as involved from the very beginning.

Jesus Christ Himself, speaking to John from heaven after His resurrection and ascension, interprets these Isaiah passages for us:

"I am Alpha and Omega, the beginning and the ending, saith the Lord, which is, and which was, and which is to come, the Almighty" (Rev. 1:8). "Saying, I am Alpha and Omega, the first and the last" (v. 11a). "Fear not; I am the first and the last: I am he that liveth, and was dead; and, behold, I am alive for evermore, Amen; and have the keys of hell and of death" (vv. 17b-18). "These things saith the first and the last, which **was dead and is alive**" (2:8). "I am Alpha and Omega, the beginning and the end, the first and the last" (22:13).

Micah 5:2, in foretelling the Incarnation of Christ, affirms that His "goings forth have been from of old, from **everlasting**" [defined by Strong as . . . the *vanishing* point; generally time *out of mind* (past or future) i.e. practically *eternity*]. Luther's German translation and several others do say "from the days of eternity," or eternity past. The New Testament presents Christ as "having neither beginning of days, nor end of life" (Heb. 7:3).

Jesus Christ is not a created being. Through Isaiah He revealed Himself as the First and the Last. Through Micah He revealed His goings forth in eternity past. His pre-existence is declared by the Apostle John, and verified in the Revelation by the Alpha and Omega Himself. He was not only *in* the beginning, He *was* the beginning.

The Holy Spirit has revealed through John that Jesus Christ the Word had been **with** God—yea, even **was** God—jointly with the Father from the very beginning (John 1:1-3).

> "In the *beginning* was the Word, and the Word was with God, and the Word was God. The same was in the *beginning* with God" (John 1:1, 2). "That which was from the *beginning,* which we have heard, which we have seen with our eyes, which we have looked upon, and our hands have handled, of the Word of life; . . . and truly our fellowship is with the Father, and with his Son Jesus Christ" (I John 1:1, 3b).

Then, approximately 4,000 years after the Creation, one-third of the Godhead voluntarily condescended from INFINITY to infancy! Yea, "the mighty El" (Isa. 9:6), who, "upholding all things by the word of his power" (Heb. 1:3), "hangeth the earth [and other planets and millions of stars] upon nothing" (Job 26:7), reduced Himself to a tiny embryo in the womb of a humble Virgin. He was born in a lowly stable, and fled for His life as a refugee to Egypt. He returned and grew to manhood in the despised little village of Nazareth (John 1:46), in a country out of which the Pharisees mistakenly said "ariseth no prophet" (7:52). (Jonah and Nahum were both from Galilee.)

Jesus condescended to reveal a holy God to fallen man, and to redeem fallen man to a gracious and holy God. His Condescension and His Virgin Birth are two miracles that have never been *outmatched*. Equaled? Yes, by His vicarious death on Calvary, and His resurrection from the dead. They will be equaled in importance once more, when His own "shall be raised incorruptible, and we shall be changed" (1 Cor. 15:51-54; Phil. 3:21):

> "For this we say unto you by the word of the Lord, that we which are alive and remain unto the coming of the Lord shall not prevent [or precede] them which are asleep. For the Lord himself shall descend from heaven with a shout, with the voice of the archangel, and the trump of God: and the dead in Christ shall rise first: then we which are alive and remain shall be caught up

together with them in the clouds, to meet the Lord in the air: and so shall we ever be with the Lord. Wherefore comfort one another with these words" (1 Thess. 4:15-18).

Then, in the Revelation the same Holy Spirit revealed this same Jesus as Master in control of End Time events. John, exiled to the lonely Isle of Patmos "for the word of God, and for the testimony of Jesus Christ" (Rev. 1:9), was used of God to reveal these truths to us. Consider what he saw, and notice our Lord's five wonderful names, plus one that no man knows.

"And I saw heaven opened, and behold a white horse; and he that sat upon him was called **Faithful** and **True**, and in righteousness he doth judge and make war. His eyes were as a flame of fire, and on his head were many crowns; and he had a **name** written, that no man knew, but he himself. And he was clothed with a vesture dipped in blood: and his name [*notice*] is called **The Word of God.**

And the armies which were in heaven followed him upon white horses, clothed in fine linen, white and clean. And out of his mouth goeth a sharp sword, that with it he might smite the nations: and he shall rule them with a rod of iron: and he treadeth the winepress of the fierceness and wrath of Almighty God. And he hath on his vesture and on his thigh a name written, **KING OF KINGS,** AND **LORD OF LORDS**" (Rev. 19:11-16).

While we do not understand everything about the future, one thing we can know: Christ is the Alpha and Omega—our hope and assurance from A to Z. He is the First and the Last—the Author and Finisher of our faith (Heb. 12:2). His death, resurrection, and ascension confirm our faith. He is the **Beginning** [the Architect of the Creation]; He is our Savior, Lord and Master today; and will be the **Ending** [the Engineer of the Consummation]. "Even so, Come, Lord Jesus"!

2

SEEING CHRIST IN THE CREATION

Glimpses of His pre-incarnate Glory which He had
with the Father before the world was. John 17:5

"In the beginning God [Elohim] **created** the heaven and the earth" (Gen. 1:1). Elohim is a plural noun which we shall consider more thoroughly in our next chapter. In this chapter we are observing glimpses of the glory of Christ in the Creation story. Some people think of God the Father as the sole Creator. But the New Testament sheds divinely inspired light on Christ's involvement in the Creation.

> "All things were made by him; and without him was not any thing made that was made. . . . He was in the world, and the world was made by him, and the world knew him not. . . . And the **Word was made flesh, and dwelt among us,** (and we beheld his glory, the glory as of the only begotten of the Father,) full of grace and truth" (John 1:3, 10, 14).

> "But to us there is but one God, the Father, of whom are all things, and we in him; and one Lord Jesus Christ, **by whom are all things, and we by him**" (1 Cor. 8:6).

> "God . . . **created all things by Jesus Christ**" (Eph. 3:9b). "For we are his workmanship, created in Christ Jesus unto good works" (Eph. 2:10a).

> ". . . for by him [by our Lord Jesus Christ] were all things created, that are in heaven, and that are in earth, visible and invisible, whether they be thrones, or dominions, or principali-

ties, or powers: all things were created by him and for him: and he is before all things, and by him all things consist. And he is the head of the body, the church: who is the beginning, **the first-born from the dead** [*the Father was never dead*]; that in all things he might have the preeminence. For it pleased the Father that in him [in Christ] should all fulness dwell" (Col. 1:15-19).

"God . . . hath in these last days spoken to us by his Son, whom he hath appointed heir of all things, **by whom also he made the worlds**" (Heb. 1:1a, 2). "But unto the Son he saith, Thy throne O God, is for ever and ever: . . . **And**, thou, Lord, in the beginning hast laid the foundation of the earth; and the heavens are the works of thine hands: . . . And as a vesture shalt thou fold them up, and they shall be changed: but thou art the same, and thy years shall not fail" (1:8a, 10, 12).

Hebrews 1:8-12 are quotations from Psalm 45:6, 7 and Psalm 102:25-27, but the writer to the Hebrews, by divine inspiration, says both passages were said *to the Son.* Therefore, every time the Bible says God *created,* we have another glimpse of Jesus' pre-incarnate glory, because we recognize by the Scriptures that the work was done *by the Father through the Son.*

Both the Hebrew *roshe* and the Greek *arche* (here translated *beginning)* have compound meanings. Strong's definition includes beginning, captain, chapiter, chief, head, ruler, principal; the first in place, time, order, or rank; the chief or principal thing.

Webster says architect is from the Greek [*architekton; archi-*, chief + *tekton*, worker]. The Bible plainly tells us that Jesus Christ is the one "by whom also he made the worlds" (Heb. 1:2), and that He is "the beginning [*the arche*] of the creation of God" (Rev. 3:14). Therefore many of us believe that rather than being a product of creation, Christ was the Chief Worker, or *Architect*, of the creation (John 1:3, 10; 1 Cor. 8:6; Eph. 3:9b; Col. 1:15-19; Heb. 1:8-12).

Genesis 1:2 briefly mentions the Spirit of God, who "moved upon the face of the waters." He is the third member of the Trinity. His role is not clearly defined here, but it is evident that He as well participated in the Creation. Perhaps His protective presence hovering over the waters, had a brooding effect, emitting life-giving energy for the waters to "bring forth abundantly the moving creature that hath life" (v.20). According to verse 26 all three participated in making man. The Spirit especially must have been involved when Elohim (the plural God) breathed into man's nostrils the breath of life, making Him a trichotomy of spirit, soul, and body (2:7).

"And God **said**, Let there be light: and there was light" (1:3). Ten times in Genesis One our Creation teacher *flashes* across the screen those three words, "and God said." What did God use each time *God said*? He used the **Word,** did He not? John says the Word was with God, and the Word was God. . . . All things were made by him; and without him was not any thing made that was made" (John 1:1, 3). It was that **Word** who "was made flesh and dwelt among us" (1:14). Obviously it was our Lord Jesus Christ!

Christ was the true Light, which lighteth every man that cometh into the world" (John 1:6-9). Therefore, since the sun, moon and stars were not created until the fourth day, the Light that was created on the first day may have been a special foreshadow of Christ, our spiritual light. Many passages speak of Christ as the Light of the world (Isa. 9:2; John 1:4; 8:12; 12:35, 46; 2 Cor. 4:6; Eph. 5:14; 1 John 2:8). Our sun today typifies Christ (Ps. 19:4b-6). And the Lamb (Jesus Christ) will be the Light of the eternal heavenly city (Rev. 21:23).

"And God said, . . . Let the dry land appear: and it was so" (Gen. 1:9). Where did it come from? It came up out of that watery mass. "And God said, Let the earth bring forth grass, the herb yielding seed, and the fruit tree yielding fruit after his kind, whose seed was in itself, upon the earth: and it was so" (v.11). Every spring when the dead grass turns green and the bare trees put on their foliage, it typifies **resurrection**—life out of death.

Do you think it was merely a coincidence that this happened for the first time on the third day? I am persuaded that God by design had carefully planned for this to take place specifically on the third creation day. Ten times we read that Jesus told His disciples He would rise from the dead on the third day (Mt. 16:21; 17:23; 20:19; 27:63; Mark 9:31; 10:34; Luke 9:22; 18:33; 24:7, 46). This *third-day* resurrection figure is a vital reminder of Him who said, "**I am the resurrection,** and the life: he that believeth in me, though he were dead, yet shall he live" (John 11:25). **The Resurrection** is beautifully illustrated in Genesis 1:9-13.

On the sixth day God said, "Let *us* make man in *our* image, after *our* likeness" (Gen. 1:26)? He surely did not say that to the angels. They are the *servants* of mankind, not their creators. Angels cannot create; in fact, they can't even pro-create—reproduce their own kind. Much less could they create a species that eventually "shall judge angels" (1 Cor. 6:3). God must have spoken to His Co-creators, His Co-partners in the Trinity. Those three plural pronouns (Gen. 1:26) are three additional glimpses of Christ's participation in the Creation.

Another reminder *flashes* across the Inspired Screen when we read that "God created man in his own **image**, in the **image** of God created he him" (Gen. 1:27). Man at his very best is only a dim foreshadow of Christ, "who is the **image** of the invisible God" (Col. 1:15; 2 Cor. 4:4b).

> Adam "is the *figure* of him [Christ] that was to come" (Rom. 5:14b), but Christ is "the brightness of [God's] glory, and the **express image** of his person (Heb. 1:3).

Instead of *flash cards*, Genesis One uses *flash words*— *Glimpses of Christ in Glory* participating with the Father in the Creation. Let's see how many such flash words we have.

Beginning (Christ is the Alpha)	1 time
Elohim (plurality includes Him)	31 times
Created (all things by Him)	5 "
God Said (Employing *the Word*)	10 "
Made (all things *made* by Him)	5 "

Light (Christ is the True Light)	10	"
Resurrection (typified)	1	"
Us, Our, Our (all three in 1:26)	3	"
Image (He is the express image)	3	"

69 words in Genesis One that reflect Christ.

Sixty-nine reminders of Jesus flashed across the Inspired Screen in the first 31 verses! Not every page has as many glimpses of Christ as Genesis One, but He shows up on page after page. Let us sit up and take notice of the Glory which He had with the Father before the world was.

Part II

Seeing Christ
in
Hebrew Names of God

3

SEEING CHRIST IN ELOHIM AND EL

Glimpses of His pre-incarnate Glory, which He had
with the Father before the world was. John 17:5

The Hebrew names of God recorded in our Bibles, are a
fascinating study. They all apply to the same God, but each
name especially emphasizes certain attributes of His character.

I. ELOHIM, THE GOD OF STRENGTH AND POWER

ELOHIM (# 430 in Strong's Concordance, see Preface
and Bibliography) is the first name by which God revealed
Himself to us in the Bible. That name appears thirty-five
times in the first thirty-four verses of Genesis. In the ordinary
sense elohim is also used for false gods ["that are no gods,"
but "the work of men's hands"–2 Chron. 13:9c; 2 Kings
19:18], and "occasionally applied by way of deference to
magistrates."

But the true Elohim is strikingly distinguished from
pagan gods by such terms as "the God of heaven" twenty-
three times, and "the God of Israel" two hundred times (compounded as LORD God [Jehovah Elohim] of Israel 108
times). "For the LORD your God is **God** of gods, and **Lord** of
lords, a great God [El], a mighty, and a terrible, which
regardeth not persons, nor taketh rewards" (Dt. 10:17).

ELOHIM, used specifically for the Supreme God, emphasizes His omnipotence and sovereignty, His power to govern, to make long range plans and fulfill them, to do whatsoever He wills. Elohim created the universe out of nothing, hung the earth upon nothing (Job 26:7), set the planets in orbit as it pleased Him, and controls them in their order to this day and forever.

"Power belongeth unto *Elohim*" (Ps. 62:11), who "by his strength setteth fast the mountains; being girded with power" (Ps. 65:6). "He divideth the sea with his power" (Job 26:12). "Our God is in the heavens: he hath done whatsoever he hath pleased" (Ps. 115:3), "for with God nothing shall be impossible" (Luke 1:37).

Elohim Demonstrates Unity in Plurality

Elohim is the plural of *El*, just like Baalim is plural for Baal (# 1168). El occurs 225 times in the Old Testament; and Elohim, 2,605 times. Eloah (# 433), chiefly found in poetry, is a singular form meaning the same as El, and appears 56 times.. Elahh (# 426, the Chaldean form used in Ezra and Daniel) corresponds with Eloah, and is found 49 times. But the plural form (Elohim) is used nearly eight times more often than the singular. The Trinity always functioned in perfect unity. Even while here on earth in the flesh, Jesus always did what pleased the Father (John 8:29).

Elohim is second in frequency to Jehovah (# 3068), which occurs 6,528 times. The four main names beginning with El are all translated God. *Jehovah* is translated either LORD or GOD (all capital letters in KJV, NKJV, and NASB). NIV uses Sovereign LORD instead of Lord GOD.

"The LORD our God is *one* LORD" [literally, Jehovah our Elohim is *one* Jehovah] (Dt. 6:4), meaning that there is no other. Strong defines the word *one* (*echad* # 259) as meaning something that is "properly *united*, i.e. *one* . . . " It is a completely unified plurality. For example, husband and wife: "and they *twain* shall be *one* flesh" (Gen. 2:24; Mark 10:8). The Holy Trinity is perfectly *united, unified* and *harmonized* such as no two human beings can possibly be.   The Father, Son, and Holy Spirit are co-eternal and co-equal, the same in substance but distinguishable in subsistence (not a tri-theism [three separate gods] but a Tri-unity).

Elohim is a Tri-unity

The Bible reveals their organizational functions as follows:

THE FATHER is essentially the SOURCE of the Divine Nature, the INITIATOR and general DIRECTOR , as we perceive by the following passages.

- "For he whom God hath sent speaketh the words of God: for God giveth not the Spirit by measure unto him. The Father loveth the Son, and hath given all things into his hand" (John 3:34, 35).

- "If I judge, my judgment is true: for I am not alone, but I and the Father that sent me" (John 8:16).

- "He that believeth on me, believeth not on me, but on him that sent me. And he that seeth me seeth him that sent me" (John 12:44, 45).

- "For I have not spoken of myself; but the Father which sent me, he gave me a commandment, what I should say, and what I should speak" (John 12:49).

THE SON is essentially the MANIFESTATION of God, and His ADMINISTRATOR.

- "Thou shalt call his name JESUS: for he shall save his people from their sins" (Mt.1:21)

- "Call his name **Emmanuel**, which being interpreted is, **God** with us" (Mt. 1:23).

- "The Word was made flesh, and dwelt among us, (and we beheld his glory, the glory as of the only begotten of the Father,) full of grace and truth" (John 1:14).

- "No man hath seen the Father at any time; the only begotten Son; which is in the bosom of the Father, he hath declared him" (John 1:18; 6:46; 1 John 4:12a).

- "And all things are of God, who hath reconciled us to himself **by Jesus Christ,** . . . To wit, that God was in Christ, reconciling the world unto himself" (2 Cor. 5: 18, 19).

- "God created all things **by Jesus Christ**" (Eph. 3:9).

- "And he [Christ] is before all things, and by him all things consist [hold together]. And he is the head of the body, the church" (Col. 1:17-18a).

- "For in him [in Christ] dwelleth all the fulness of the Godhead bodily" (Col. 2:9).

- "Whom he hath appointed heir of all things, and by whom also he made the worlds; who being the brightness of his glory, and the express image of his person, and upholding all things by the word of his power, when he had by himself purged our sins, sat down on the right hand of the Majesty on high" (Heb. 1:2-3).

THE SPIRIT is essentially the ENERGY of Divine Nature, through Whom the Trinity works.

- "In the beginning God created the heaven and the earth. And the earth was without form, and void; . . . and the **Spirit** of God moved upon the face of the waters" (Gen. 1:1, 2). [Undoubtedly it was by the energy of the Spirit that the waters brought "forth abundantly the moving creature that hath life, and fowl that may fly . . ."–Gen. 1:20].

- "But if the Spirit of him that raised up Jesus from the dead dwell in you, he that raised up Christ from the dead shall also quicken your mortal bodies by his Spirit that dwelleth in you" (Rom. 8:11).

- Paul did "mighty signs and wonders, by the power of the Spirit of God" (Rom. 15:19).

- "And my speech and my preaching was . . . in demonstration of the Spirit of Power."

- "But we all with open face beholding as in a glass the glory of the Lord, are changed into the same image from glory to glory, even as by the Spirit of the Lord" (2 Cor. 3:18). [The above verses, and others, reveal the Holy Spirit as the energy by which the marvelous works of God are accomplished.]

Not only do the members of the Trinity work each in His own role, but they are capable of overlapping and working interchangeably as well, as we shall see in the following verses.

*A. Each of the Three is called **God**:*
1. Father: "Peace from **God** our Father" (Rom. 1:7).
2. *Son: "Emmanuel . . . **God** with us" (Mt. 1:23); Isaiah 9:6; Romans 9:5; Hebrews 1:8.
3. Spirit: By lying "to the Holy Ghost . . [Ananias lied] unto **God**" (Acts 5:3, 4).

*B. Each of the Three is called **Lord***:
1. Father: "**Lord** of heaven and earth" (Mt. 11:25).
2. Son: "God made Jesus ... **Lord** and Christ" (Acts 2:36). "If thou shalt confess . . . the **Lord** Jesus" (Rom. 10:9).
3. Spirit: "Now the **Lord** is that Spirit, . . . " (2 Cor. 3:17).

*C. Each of the Three is called **Creator**:*
1. Father: "Have we not all one father? hath not one God created us?" (Mal. 2:10)
2. *Son: John 1:3, 10; Colossians 1:15-19 ; Hebrews 1:2.
3. Spirit: "The Spirit of God hath made me" (Job 33:4).

*D. Each of the Three is called **Comforter**:*
1. Father: ". . . the Father . . . God of all comfort" (2 Cor. 1:3)
2. *Son: John 14:18; Philippians 2:1; 2 Thessalonians 2:16, 17.
3. Spirit: "The Comforter, which is the Holy Ghost" (John 14:26).
* For the Son there were too many references to quote them all. Look them up and read them.

II. EL, THE MOST HIGH GOD, the ALMIGHTY

El (# 410) is a singular name for the same God. That name first appears in Genesis 14:18-22. In those five verses it appears four times, each time compounded with the descriptive title, Elyon (# 5945), meaning **most high.** *El Elyon (God most High)*, translated in reverse order, is "the most high God." That exact title is found eight times in the Old Testament and three times in the New Testament. The adjective then became a superlative proper noun, **"the most High,"** used 30 times in the Old Testament to describe God—eleven times in the Psalms. For example:

"He that dwelleth in the secret place of **the most High** shall abide under the shadow of the Almighty" (Ps. 91:1).

"Because thou hast made the LORD, *which is* my refuge, *even* **the most High,** thy habitation; There shall no evil befall thee, neither shall any plague come nigh thy dwelling" (Ps. 91:9-10).

"It is **God [El]** that girdeth me with **strength,** and maketh my way perfect" (18:32).

"The heavens declare the **glory** of **God [El]**; and the firmament sheweth his **handywork**" (19:1).

Strong defines the name El as meaning "strength, (adj.) *mighty,* especially the *Almighty.*" The singular name does not deny His undivided Triunity, but rather emphasizes His unique position as "the most High." He far transcends the comprehension of natural man. That is why the cults deny His Triunity.

In Genesis 21:33 He is called "the everlasting El." In 31:13 He said to Jacob, "I am the El of Bethel, where thou anointedst the pillar, and where thou vowedst a vow unto me: now arise, get thee out from this land [Haran], and return unto the land of thy kindred [Canaan]." God was telling Jacob, "I, the Mighty God, yea, the Almighty God, will be with you."

When Jacob's whole family was migrating to Egypt, "Elohim spake unto Israel in the visions of the night, and said, Jacob, Jacob. . . . I am **El**, the **Elohim** of thy father: fear not to go down into Egypt; for I will there make of thee a great nation: I will go down with thee into Egypt; and I will also surely bring thee up again: and Joseph shall put his hand upon thine eyes" (Gen. 46:2-4).

When the children of Israel had come through the Red sea on dry ground they sang a song of victory, saying, "Jehovah is my strength and song, and he is become my salvation: he is my **El**, and I will prepare him an habitation; my father's **Elohim**, and I will exalt him" (Ex. 15:2). El and Elohim are two descriptive names for the same God.

El is definitely used to identify Jesus Christ, as well as the Father. "For unto us a child is born, unto us a son is given: and the government shall be upon his shoulder: and his name shall be called Wonderful, Counsellor, **The mighty God** [El], **The everlasting Father**, The Prince of Peace" (Isa. 9:6). We all know that this El (translated **The mighty God**) was the Son.

Why call the Son "The everlasting Father"? Luther's German, and at least two other translators say "Eternal Father." "Literally the words mean the 'Father of eternity,' One who in His own being is eternal and is thus able to give the gift of eternal life to others" (The New Bible Commentary, 1963). On that basis it was very logical for Jesus to call His disciples, "Little children" (John 13:33). From eternity past He was designated to be our Savior, our spiritual Father. And, while the Old Testament is "the book of the generations [plural] of Adam" (Gen. 5:1), the New Testament is "The book of the generation [sing.] of Jesus Christ" (Mt. 1:1). He has no grandchildren.

Isaiah, by divine inspiration, very accurately foretold the virgin birth of Christ, and called His name **Immanuel** (7:14), approximately seven hundred and forty years before His first advent. Matthew reports the fulfillment of that prophecy, and by divine inspiration interprets the name for us: "Call his name **Emmanuel,** which being interpreted is, **God with us**" (Mt. 1:23).

After the Babylonian captivity Nehemiah spoke of Israel's frequent rebellion against God. Then he added, "But thou art a God [Eloah] ready to pardon, gracious and merciful, slow to anger, and of great kindness, and forsookest them not" (Neh. 9:17b). Pardon is available to fallen mankind ONLY through the Lord Jesus Christ.

In this chapter we have **El, Eloah, El Elyon, Elohim, Jehovah, Emmanuel.** They are six names of Deity given to our Lord Jesus Christ by divine inspiration. They declare some of the glory which Jesus had with the Father before the world was.

4

SEEING CHRIST IN JEHOVAH

Glimpses of His pre-incarnate Glory, which He had
with the Father before the world was. John 17:5.

JEHOVAH (# 3068 in Strong's Concordance) is perhaps
the highest and most awesome of all the Hebrew names of
God. It is also the most frequent, occurring 6,528 times in the
Old Testament. The Jews considered it so holy they feared to
pronounce it. The name *Jehovah* emphasizes His eternal self-
existence ("having neither beginning of days nor end of life"),
as well as His moral attributes such as holiness, righteousness, love, mercy, grace, and justice. *Elohim,* as indicated in
Chapter Three, denotes His sovereignty and strength, His
ability to do whatsoever He wills.

Jehovah (in the King James and several other English
versions) is translated LORD or GOD (all capital letters), to
distinguish it from His other names. It appears for the first
time in Genesis 2:4, as **LORD** God (Jehovah Elohim). That
combination occurs 20 times in chapters 2 and 3, always in
connection with something Jehovah was doing especially for
the good of man. In fact the combination "LORD God"
(Jehovah Elohim) is found 532 times in the Bible.

The significance of the name Jehovah was not fully
revealed to man until He was preparing to deliver His people
out of Egypt. At that time God said to Moses, "I am the
LORD: and I appeared unto Abraham, unto Isaac, and unto
Jacob, by the name of God Almighty [El-Shaddai], but by my

name JEHOVAH was I not known to them" (Ex. 6:2-3). The name Jehovah appears 160 times in Genesis, but we must realize that Moses wrote Genesis *after* that revelation at the burning bush.

Jehovah is the God of *revelation* and *redemption.* That name certainly includes Jesus Christ. He is God's ultimate *revelation* of Himself to man, and the very One through whom God *redeems* man to Himself. Christ is the bridge, the connecting link, between God and man.

Satan, in tempting Eve, spoke of *Elohim* but not of *Jehovah;* and Eve did the same in answering Satan (Gen. 3:1b-5). But *Jehovah Elohim is* named eight times when He came to clothe them, seeking their rescue (vv. 8-23).

It was for their protection that God sent man forth from the Garden, "lest he put forth his hand, and take also of the tree of life, and eat, and live forever [in their fallen state]" (3. 22b). Before He sent them out, He explained the consequences of their disobedience, but promised them a Seed who would eventually bruise the serpent's head (Satan) and make salvation possible (v. 15).

It was Jehovah who accepted Abel's offering, and called Cain into account for his sin. It was Jehovah who "saw that the wickedness of man was great in the earth, and that every imagination of the thought of his heart was only evil continually" (Gen. 6:5).

Genesis 6:5 is the first time Jehovah is translated GOD. A few King James publishers fail to show GOD in capital letters here. Several versions translate it LORD (all capital letters). The New Jerusalem Bible uses Yahweh. Strong, and several other reliable sources indicate that the original word is what we call Jehovah in English. It seems logical that Jehovah (the God of Redemption), seeing the overwhelming wickedness, would do something about it.

Jehovah and *Elohim*, applying to the same God, may at times be used interchangeably. But sometimes they seem to be carefully selected because of the specific attributes they emphasize. Elohim instructed Noah to make an enormous boat, and gather into it of every living thing, two of every sort, to preserve animal life on the earth. "Thus did Noah; according to all that *Elohim* commanded him, so did he" (Gen. 6:19-22).

But it was Jehovah who said unto Noah, "Come thou and all thy house into the ark" (7:1). It was Jehovah who told him to bring in of every clean beast and fowl, which were needed for their sacrifices. "And Noah did according to all that *Jehovah* commanded him" (7:2-5).

Elohim, the mighty covenant keeping God, remembered Noah and every living thing, and assuaged the waters, until the earth became dry again (8:1-5). Elohim blessed Noah, added meat to his vegetarian diet, prescribed the penalty for murder, and established the rainbow as a sign of His covenant (9:1-17). Noah blessed *Jehovah* as the God of Shem, through whose line Christ came into the flesh (9:26); but said *Elohim* shall enlarge Japheth, the father of the Gentiles (v. 27).

Jehovah found Abram among the idol worshipers at Ur of the Chaldeas, and set him apart for special blessings, as follows:

> "Get thee out of thy country, and from thy kindred, and from thy Father's house, unto a land that I will shew thee: and I will make of thee a great nation, and I will bless thee, and make thy name great; and thou shalt be a blessing: and I will bless them that bless thee, and curse him that curseth thee: and in thee shall all the families of the earth be blessed" (Gen. 12:1-3).

Concerning this, Paul says that "the scripture, foreseeing that God would justify the heathen through faith, **preached before the gospel unto Abraham,** *saying,* In thee shall all nations be blessed" (Gal 3:8). That unique Blessing was Christ, brought into the flesh through Abraham.

In Genesis 18 Jehovah appeared unto Abraham. Abraham "looked, and lo, three men stood by him" (v. 2). Quickly he prepared for them a meal, "and he stood by them under the tree, and they did eat" (v. 8). "And the men rose up . . . and went toward Sodom: but Abraham stood yet before the LORD" (vv. 16-22). His pleading with Jehovah for sparing the righteous—in case He finds 50, or 40, or 30, or 20, or even 10 righteous persons in Sodom—is a familiar story.

Throughout the chapter, five times (vv. 3, 27, 30, 31,32) Abraham addressed his heavenly visitor as *Lord* (Adonai); but Moses in the same chapter identified him as LORD (Jehovah) ten times (vv. 1, 13, 14, 17, 19, 19, 20, 22, 26, 33). Abraham certainly saw this Man face to face, whom Moses clearly identified as Jehovah. Unless we recognize this and all other Old Testament theophanies (*appearances of God*) as Christophanies (*appearances of the pre-incarnate Christ*), we will have a real problem with those New Testament passages that declare plainly, "No man hath seen God [*"the Father"* (John 6:46)] at any time" (John 1:18; 1 John 4:12).

I take it no mortal man has ever seen the Father except in the Person of Christ. After all, Christ is "the brightness of [God's] glory, and the **express image** of His person" (Heb. 1:3). That being the case, Jesus could well say, "He that hath seen me hath seen the Father" (John 14:9b). Truth is self-evident

Elohim tested Abraham, requesting the sacrifice of his son Isaac (Gen. 22:1, 3, 8, 9). But just as Abraham prepared to strike the fatal blow, "the angel of **Jehovah** called out of heaven, and said, Abraham, Abraham: . . . Lay not thine hand upon the lad, . . . for now I know that thou fearest God, seeing thou hast not withheld thy son, thine only son from me" (22:11, 12). "And the angel of Jehovah called . . . the second time" (vv. 15-18), and renewed His Abrahamic covenant and promise. Jesus may well have had that occasion in mind when He said, "Abraham rejoiced to see my day: and he saw it, and was glad" (John 8:56).

Jacob saw in a dream a ladder reaching from earth to heaven. "And, behold, the LORD stood above it, and said, I am the LORD God [Jehovah Elohim] of Abraham thy father, and the God of Isaac: . . ." (Gen. 28:13). Now who was this, knowing that "no man hath seen God [the Father] at any time"? It was at least a foreshadow of what Jesus said to Nathanael, "Verily, verily, I say unto you, Hereafter ye shall see heaven open, and the angels of God ascending and descending upon the **Son of man**" (John 1:51).

We come with Moses to the burning bush, and find that "the angel of the LORD appeared unto him in a flame of fire out of the midst of a bush" (Ex. 3:2). An angel is a messenger sent, but we do not find that God the Father was ever sent, or is ever called an angel of the Lord. Yet verse 4 says when *Jehovah* saw that Moses turned aside to see, *Elohim* called to him out of the midst of the bush. All three names seem to identify one and the same Person. If that was not the pre-incarnate Christ, who was it?

When Moses asked for His name, God said, "I AM THAT I AM: . . . Thus shalt thou say unto the children of Israel, **I AM** hath sent me unto you" (Ex. 3:14). And Jesus says, "Verily, verily, I say unto you, Before Abraham was, I AM" (John 8:58); and, "if ye believe not that I am *he*, ye shall die in your sins" (John 8:24). Notice in your Bible, in John 8:24, 28; and 13:19, that the pronoun *he* is in italics, meaning it was added by the translators. **Jesus Himself is the Great I AM.**

When God delivered Israel out of Egypt, "**Jehovah went before them** by day in a pillar of a cloud, to lead them the way; and by night in a pillar of fire, to give them light" (Ex. 13:21). And when the Egyptian army pursued them in the Red Sea, "**the angel of God, which went before** the camp of Israel, removed and went behind them" (14:19). "And **Jehovah** looked unto the host of the Egyptians through the pillar of fire and of the cloud, and troubled the host of the Egyptians" (v. 24). That corresponds with what the Lord said further:

> "Behold, I send an angel before thee, to keep thee in the way, and to bring thee into the place which I have prepared. Beware of him, and obey his voice, provoke him not; . . . for **my name is in him**. . . . For **mine Angel** shall go before thee" (Ex. 23:20, 21, 23a).

"And he said, **My presence** shall go with thee, and I will give thee rest" (Ex. 33:14).

"In all their affliction he was afflicted, and **the Angel of his presence** saved them: in his love and in his pity he redeemed them; and he bare them, and carried them all the days of old" (Isa. 63:9).

"For they drank of that spiritual Rock that followed them; and that Rock was Christ" (1 Cor. 10:4). And verse 9 says **they tempted Christ. Christ was the Jehovah in charge of God's people.**

Isaiah described John the Baptist as "the voice of him that crieth in the wilderness, Prepare ye the way of the LORD [Jehovah], make straight in the desert a highway for our God [Elohim]" (Isa. 40:3). And the angel, announcing John's birth to Zacharias, said, "He [John] shall go before him [Christ] in the spirit and power of Elias, to turn the hearts of the fathers to the children, and the disobedient to the wisdom of the just; to make ready a people prepared for the Lord [Kurios – namely Jesus]" (Luke 1:17; Mal. 4:5, 6). We know that John the Baptist prepared the way for our Lord Jesus Christ, the One whom Isaiah called Jehovah and Elohim. It is clearly evident that the names *Jehovah* and *Elohim* both apply to the Son, as well as to the Father.

5

SEEING CHRIST IN EL-SHADDAI

Glimpses of His pre-incarnate Glory, which He had
with the Father before the world was. John 17:5

When Abram was ninety-nine years old, and Sarai was ninety, Jehovah appeared to him again and announced, "I am the Almighty God [or God Almighty—*El-Shaddai*], walk before me, and be thou perfect." (Gen. 17:1). In other words, "Believe My promise and trust Me"! El (like Elohim) is the strong covenant keeping God. Whatever He declares or promises He will certainly do.

Shaddai, however, was a new name, which had not occurred before. It denotes abundant sufficiency regardless of how hopeless the circumstances may be; and the capability of making exceedingly fruitful (Gen. 17:6; 28:3; 35:11; 48:3-4; 49:25). *El-Shaddai* is a combination of two great names: *Shaddai* (translated *the Almighty*), preceded by *El*, the *strong* and *mighty God*. Combining the two seems to intensify them both, like the "Verily, verily," frequently used by Jesus.

Abram had long been a great man of faith, but even he suffered a few low points in his life. According to Genesis 12:1-4, he had God's promise of a son even before he left Ur of the Chaldees. We are not told how long they lived at Haran where his father died, after which Abram had already lived in Canaan for ten years, with no apparent evidence of a son by

Sarai. Unfortunately Abram yielded to Sarai's ill-contrived plan to help God make His promise good.

Their humanistic effort was a *successful failure*. Abram had a son, but he was not the son of promise, nor of Sarai. It set the stage for family conflicts (Gen. 16:1-6; 21:9-21), and for a redounding series of international conflicts that rages through the Middle East today. So God waited thirteen more years—until Abram too was "dead" (impotent). El-Shaddai fills empty vessels, just like Christ fills empty lives with spiritual fruit!

Abram got the message, and his faith sprang to life again! Even his name was changed from Abram to Abraham—"a father of many nations" (Gen. 17:5). Instead of continuing to focus on the "deadness" of their own bodies, he now trusted the life-giving power of El-Shaddai. From that time forth,

"He considered not his own body now dead [impotent], . . . neither yet the deadness of Sara's womb: he [no longer] staggered at the promise of God through unbelief; but was strong in faith, giving glory to God" (Rom. 4:19, 20).

"Through [this revival of] faith also Sara herself received strength to conceive seed, and was delivered of a child when she was past age, because she judged him faithful who had promised. Therefore sprang there even of one, and *him* [Abraham] as good as dead, so many as the stars of the sky in multitude, and as the sand which is by the sea shore innumerable" (Heb. 11:11, 12).

El-Shaddai restored functions of nature that had been dead for perhaps more than a decade. In fact, He made nature reverse itself and do that which was contrary to nature. Isaac, the long promised son was born of Sarai, exactly as El-Shaddai declared. Even so Christ reverses the fallen nature of man, enabling us to bear spiritual fruit for God.

In the next generation Isaac blessed Jacob (upon sending him to Padanaram), saying,

"*El-Shaddai* bless thee, and make thee fruitful, and multiply thee, that thou mayest be a multitude of people; and give thee the blessing of Abraham, to thee, and to thy seed with thee; that thou mayest inherit the land wherein thou art a stranger, which God gave unto Abraham" (28:3-4).

"And [when Jacob had returned to Canaan] God said unto him , I am *El-Shaddai*: be fruitful and multiply; a nation and a company of nations shall be of thee, and kings shall come out of thy loins; and the land which I gave Abraham and Isaac, to thee will I give it, and to thy seed after thee will I give the land" (Gen. 35:11, 12).

Jacob, at the close of his life blessed all his sons, each with his own peculiar blessing. Joseph he especially endowed with those three mighty names of God.

"Joseph is a fruitful bough, even a fruitful bough by a well: whose branches run over the wall: . . . and the arms of his hands were made strong by the hands of the **mighty** *God* of Jacob; . . . even by the **El** of thy father, who shall help thee; and by the **Almighty** [*Shaddai*], who shall bless thee with blessings from heaven above, blessings of the deep that lieth under, blessings of the breasts, and of the womb: the blessings of thy father have prevailed above the blessings of my progenitors unto the utmost bound of the everlasting hills: they shall be on the head of Joseph, and on the crown of the head of him that was separate from his brethren" (Gen. 49:22-26).

God said to Moses, "I appeared unto Abraham, unto Isaac, and unto Jacob, by the name of God Almighty [El-Shaddai], but by my name Jehovah was I not known to them" (Ex. 6:3). It is evident, however, that they used the name Jehovah occasionally. Perhaps the meaning is that He had not yet revealed the full significance of His name Jehovah.

Since Job may have been contemporary with Abraham, his book is older than Genesis. In Job we find El 53 times; Eloah 40 times; and Elohim 17 times. Right now we are especially considering Jehovah, translated the LORD, and *Shaddai*, translated the Almighty. Each appears thirty-one times in the Book of Job.

Why, and by whom, was that name Shaddai used so often when Job was suffering so nigh unto death? Did Job's friends use it to comfort Job, or to reprimand him? Since Shaddai denotes abundant sufficiency, even in the most dire circumstances, it could and should have been used kindly, as a healing balm for Job, who was broken beyond recognition (Job 2:12).

Eliphaz used it seven times (5:17; 15:25; 22:3, 17, 23, 25, 26), Bildad twice (8:3, 5), Zophar once (11:7), Elihu six times (32:8; 33:4; 34:10, 12; 35:13; 37:23), God once (40:2), and Job used it fourteen times, a few times indiscreetly. We must consider the pain and strain Job was suffering, so that he described his own words as "the speeches of one that is desperate, which are as wind" (Job 6:26).

Job's "miserable comforters" (16:2) all showed a high respect for the Almighty [Shaddai], even when speaking quite harshly to Job. For example:

"Doth the Almighty pervert justice" (8:3)? "If thou wouldest . . . make thy supplication to the Almighty; . . . surely he would awake for thee . . ." (8:5-6). "If thou return to the Almighty, thou shalt be built up" (22:23). "Yea, the Almighty shall be thy defence, and thou shalt have plenty of silver" (22:25). "The inspiration of the Almighty giveth understanding" (32:8). "The breath of the Almighty hath given me life" (33:4). "Far be it from God, that he should do wickedness; and from the Almighty, that he should commit iniquity" (34:10). "Yea, surely God will not do wickedly, neither will the Almighty pervert judgment" (34:12). "Touching the Almighty, we cannot find him out: he is excellent in power, and in judgment, and in plenty of justice: he will not afflict" (37:23). Then we have the keynote from God Himself, "Shall he that contendeth with the Almighty instruct him? he that reproveth God, let him answer it" (40:2).

Notice a few statements by Job himself. Job 6:14 is variously translated in different versions. Some say that he who withholds comfort forsakes godly fear; others see the afflicted as in danger of forsaking the fear of God because no one comforts them. It may be both.

"To him that is afflicted pity should be shewed from his friend; but he forsaketh the fear of the Almighty" (KJV).

"For the dispairing man there should be kindness from his friend; lest he forsake the fear of the Almighty" (NASB).

"Whoever holds back kindness from a fainting friend, he abandons his reverence for the Almighty" (Berkeley).

Job asks, "Will [the hypocrite] delight himself in the Almighty? will he always call upon God" (27:10).   Job yearned for the former days: "When the Almighty was yet with me, when my children were about me" (29:5). "Oh that one would hear me! behold, my desire is, that the Almighty would answer me, and that mine adversary had written a book" (31:35). Shaddai did answer Job.   When his unique calamity was over, Job's emptied life overflowed with double blessings (42:12).

We do not find any of Job's friends mentioning the name Jehovah (the God of Revelation and Redemption) It appears 17 times in Job 1 and 2, once in 12:9 by Job himself, and 13 times in chapters 38 through 42, in the dialog between the LORD and Job. Job used the name Adonai (# 136) once (Lord, small o-r-d), in 28:28. Apparently His name Jehovah was not yet well known, nor its significance well understood in Job's day.

The name Shaddai was known to Balaam. Balaam sought to curse Israel because he "loved the wages of unrighteousness" (2 Pet. 2:15), but he was overruled by God. Four times he tried to curse them, but he could not. The last two times he confessed that he "saw the vision of the Almighty [*Shaddai*], falling into a trance, but having his eyes open" (Nu. 24:4, 16). Each time He could only bless and not curse. The Almighty (Shaddai) was in control watching over Israel. Was not He "that spiritual Rock that followed them [?]: and that Rock was Christ" (1 Cor. 10:4).

In the final analysis we find the meaning of these Hebrew names for God ultimately demonstrated and fulfilled in the very Person of Jesus Christ. Christ is the true Vine, the divine

Source of spiritual fruitfulness (John 15:1-8). Without Christ we are as barren of spiritual fruit as Sarah was of physical seed, until El-Shaddai showered them with His blessings.

And, as suggested earlier, any visible appearances of God were probably appearances of the pre-incarnate Christ, because "no man hath seen God [the Father] at any time" (John 1:18; 6:46;   1 John 4:12). Those Old Testament Christophanies are shining glimpses of Christ's pre-incarnate glory still reflected from the pages of Old Testament history!

6

SEEING CHRIST IN ADONAI

Glimpses of His pre-incarnate Glory, which He had
with the Father before the world was. John 17:5

The Bible uses more than a dozen different Hebrew
names to reveal the all-sufficiency of God. Each name
emphasizes some specific aspect of His Person, character, or
work. In former chapters we have seen that *Elohim* denotes
His sovereignty and the power to do whatsoever He wills.
Jehovah emphasizes His moral attributes, such as holiness,
righteousness, love, and redemption. *El-Shaddai* depicts Him
as the super-abundant Supplier of every need, the Source and
controller of nature itself, even making nature do what is contrary to nature.

In this chapter we are considering *Adonai,* translated Lord
(small o-r-d), or Sovereign LORD in New International
Version. Either one emphasizes His **divine Lordship**.
Adonai is found 432 times in the Old Testament. Our Adonai
is the divine, legal **Owner** and **Master** of all human beings,
as well as of the possessions He entrusts to us.

The Hebrew word for *human* masters is adon (# 113).
Adon occurs 331 times in the Old Testament, frequently
translated master. Adonai (# 136), applying to Deity, is
defined by Strong as "an emphatic form of 113; the *Lord*
(used as a proper noun for God only):— (my) Lord." "Used

of men it is always in the singular form, *adon.* Only of God is it in the plural."[1]

Adonai appears for the first time in Genesis 15:2. Four kings had overpowered five kings, and had taken captive all the people of Sodom, including Lot and his family. Abram had undertaken a rescue, and miraculously recovered everything. Melchizedek, the king of Salem and priest of the most high God, brought bread and wine and blessed Abram.

After Abram had rejected the rewards offered by the king of Sodom, the LORD (Jehovah) appeared to him in a vision, saying. "Fear not, Abram: I am thy shield, and thy exceeding great reward." Unflattered by all this recognition, Abram there revealed the inner yearning of his heart, pleading, "Lord GOD [**Adonai Jehovah**], what wilt thou give me, seeing I go childless?" By addressing God as Adonai he submissively acknowledged Him as his **Sovereign Master.**

Abram understood well the role of a servant, as well as that of a godly master. Just a few verses earlier (Gen. 14:14), we see that Abram had more than three hundred "trained servants" of his own. He had a good relationship with his servants. Many of them were "born in his own house," and were permanent members of his household. He provided and cared for them as though they were his own children. One of them, "Eliezer of Damascus" (15:2), was the steward of Abram's house.

Eliezer (intentionally unnamed) was undoubtedly the servant sent by Abram to bring a wife for Isaac. Typifying the Holy Spirit, he did "not speak of himself" (John 16:13), but he spoke much, and very highly, of his master and his master's son. Eighteen times in this account (Genesis 24), Abraham is portrayed as a highly esteemed master (*adon*). Abraham typifies God the Father providing a Bride for His beloved Son, Jesus Christ. (Discussed in chapter nineteen, *Seeing Christ Typified in Abraham and Isaac.*)

---

[1]Taken from *Names of God,* by Nathan Stone, p. 44. Copyright 1944. Moody Bible Institute of Chicago Moody Press. Used with permission.

Moses, when called of God to deliver Israel from Egypt, felt inadequate and fearful. He said, "O my Lord [Adonai], I am not eloquent, . . . O my Lord [Adonai], send . . . whom thou wilt send [anyone else, but not me]" (Ex. 4:10, 13). Twice he confessed God as his Master but resisted His orders, and God's anger was kindled (v. 14). However, when Moses yielded, Adonai clothed him with miraculous power, used him marvelously in forty years of active service, and "Moses was faithful in all his house" (Heb. 3:2). Jesus Christ (Dt. 18:15, 18) is called "a prophet . . . *like unto Moses*, whom the LORD knew face to face" (Dt.34:10).

The Psalmists rejoiced in Adonai!   Sixty times they addressed Him by that title, proclaiming Him as their assurance, hope, and joy. (Adonai is the Hebrew word translated Lord.)

- "O LORD our Adonai, how excellent is thy name in all the earth !" (8:1).

- "Thou art my Adonai; *I know of no good apart from Thee*" (16:2, so the German).

- "For in thee, O LORD, do I hope: thou wilt hear, O Adonai Elohim" (38:15).

- "For I am poor and needy: yet Adonai thinketh upon me: . . ." (40:17)

- "Blessed be Adonai, who daily loadeth us with benefits, . . ." (68:19).

- "For thou art my hope, O Adonai Jehovah: for thou art my trust from my youth" (71:5).

- "I have put my trust in Adonai Jehovah, that I may declare all thy works" (73:28b).

- "Jehovah said to my Adonai, Sit thou at my right hand, until I make thine enemies my footstool" (110:1).

The combination Lord GOD (Adonai Jehovah), in contrast to LORD God (Jehovah Elohim), appears most often after Israel's Babylonian captivity.   LORD God (Jehovah

Elohim) occurs 226 times in the Old Testament *but only 18 times after the Psalms.* Lord GOD (Adonai Jehovah) occurs 302 times in all, only 19 times before Isaiah, *but 217 times in Ezekiel alone.* See columns at the end of this chapter.

Adonai distinguishes God as Owner and Master of all people. Owning people is known as slavery, which to us savors of tyranny. But every one of us is *servant* (bond slave) to a master, whether we know it or not. Our eternal destiny depends on whether we serve God or Satan.

Slave owners bought and sold their bond servants as personal property. (Unfortunately that is still practiced in some places.) Adonai Jehovah had made an enormous investment in Israel. They were His "peculiar treasure" (Ex. 19:5; Ps. 135:4), "his special . . . peculiar people" (Dt. 7:6; 14:2; 26:18), "whom he hath chosen for his own inheritance" (1 Kings 8:53; Ps. 33:12).

Israel was no longer content to be a unique theocracy. They requested to "be like all the nations; and that our king may judge us, and go out before us, and fight our battles" (1 Sam. 8:20). In addition to demanding a king, they also forsook their Adonai and worshipped the gods of other nations. They "changed their glory for that which doth not profit" (Jer. 2:11), "the work of their own hands, that which their own fingers have made" (Isa. 2:8). Since they insisted on being like other nations, God sold them to Nebuchadnezzar, a mighty king of many nations.

Israel, as well as we, are God's *personal property.* He has the right to do with all of us what He knows needs to be done for our spiritual welfare, and for the fulfillment of His eternal plan. We are all equally dependent upon our Triune God. He is our Creator, Preserver, and Redeemer.

Ezekiel had been carried to Babylon as a young man, and was called to the prophetic ministry, and apparently the priesthood, five years later (Ezek. 1:1-3). He prophesied as a captive in Babylon, but his messages included conditions and activities at Jerusalem. He denounced false doctrine and pled for repentance. His frequent use of the name **Adonai** gives recognition to the Lordship of God, even acknowledging God's right to sell them to Nebuchadnezzar. But there is more.

Ezekiel did not stop with Adonai alone. His use of **Lord GOD** (Adonai compounded with Jehovah) 217 times, and **LORD** (Jehovah) separately 213 times, suggests that Ezekiel was looking beyond their Captivity. Focusing on **Jehovah** (the God who cleanses, pardons, redeems, and restores) he may have foreseen the deliverance that surpasses their deliverance from Egypt, as foretold by Jeremiah, who was contemporary with Ezekiel.

> "Behold, the days come, saith the LORD [Jehovah], that I will raise unto David a righteous Branch, and a King shall reign and prosper, and shall execute judgment and justice in the earth. In his days Judah shall be saved, and Israel shall dwell safely: and this *is* his name whereby he shall be called, THE LORD OUR RIGHTEOUSNESS. Therefore, behold, the days come, saith the LORD, that they shall no more say, The LORD liveth, which brought up the children of Israel out of the land of Egypt; But, The LORD liveth, which brought up and which led the seed of the house of Israel out of the north country, and from all countries whither I had driven them; and they shall dwell in their own land" (Jer. 23:5-8).

Jeremiah saw, with increasing intensity, that their captivity is not the end of Israel. Three times, in chapters four and five, he declared that the Lord "will not make a full end of [Israel]" (Jer. 4:27; 5:10, 18). Later he gets more emphatic.

> "For I am with thee, saith the LORD [Jehovah], to save thee: though I make a full end of all nations whither I have scattered thee, yet will I not make a full end of thee: . . . (Jer. 30:11).

> "Fear thou not, O Jacob my servant, saith the Lord: for I am with thee; for **I will** make a full end of all nations whither I have scattered thee [that includes the Americas]: but I will not make a full end of thee, but correct thee in measure; yet will I not leave thee wholly unpunished" (Jer. 46:28).

Their captivity and slavery administered discipline and correction, but not annihilation. God can do wonders with adverse circumstances. **Adonai Jehovah** sometimes accepts detours, but He will never be defeated! The Mosaic Law endowed purchased slaves with privileges that strangers and hired servants did not have:

> "This is the ordinance of the passover: there shall no stranger eat thereof: but every man's servant that is bought for money, when thou hast circumcised him, then shall he eat thereof. A foreigner and an hired servant shall not eat thereof" (Ex. 12:43-45).

> "There shall no stranger eat of the holy thing: a sojourner of the priest, or an hired servant, shall not eat of the holy thing. But if the priest buy any soul with his money, he shall eat of it, and he that is born in his house: they shall eat of his meat" (Lev. 22:10, 11).

Even in the early church there were Christians who were bond servants—a carry-over of early culture. Paul encouraged slaves to be faithful to their masters as a manifestation of God's grace in their life, "with good will doing service, as to the Lord, and not to men" (Eph. 6:5-8; 1 Tim. 6:1; Titus 2:9).

> "And, ye masters, do the same things unto them [your bond servants], forbearing threatening: knowing that your Master also is in heaven; neither is there respect of persons with him" (Eph. 6:9; Col. 4:1).

> "Were you a slave when you were called? Do not let that trouble you; but if a chance of liberty should come, take it. For the man who as a slave received the call to be a Christian is the Lord's freedman, and, equally, the free man who received the call is a slave in the service of Christ" (1 Cor. 7:21-22, New English Bible).

Perhaps it was for symbolic reasons that Hebrew law admitted purchased bond servants to the Passover. Only bond servants of Adonai experience a freedom which others cannot know—freedom, not to follow their flesh to their ruin, but to follow their Master to victory over Satan, sin, and self. Heaven is reserved for the Lord's bond servants..

The New Testament reveals clearly that **our Adonai is the Lord Jesus Christ Himself.** He is the One who purchased the Church with His own blood (Acts 20:28).

"What? know ye not that your body is the temple of the Holy Ghost which is in you, which ye have of God, and **ye are not your own? For ye are bought with a price:** therefore glorify God in your body, and in your spirit, which are God's" (1 Cor. 6:19, 20).

Every true Christian is the purchased possession of Jesus Christ, our **Adonai** and our **Jehovah.** Ultimately it was through Christ that God revealed Himself to man (Heb. 1:1-4), and it is through Christ that He redeems man to Himself. Only through Christ do we obtain eternal LIFE.

"Neither is there salvation in any other: for there is none other name under heaven given among men, whereby we must be saved" (Acts 4:12).

The following columns show clearly where each combination is most used.

Jehovah Elohim used *mostly* in history. Occurs first in Gen. 2:4 **Jehovah Elohim** Transl. **LORD God**		**Adonai Jehovah** used *mostly* by the Prophets. Occurs first in Gen. 5:2 **Adonai Jehovah** Transl. **Lord GOD**	
Genesis	27 times	Genesis	2 times
Exodus	12	Exodus	2
Deuteron.	8	Deuteronomy	2
Joshua	17	Joshua	1
Judges	8	Judg.	2
Ruth	1	2 Samuel	6
1 Samuel	9	1 Kings	2
2 Samuel	4	Psalms	4
1 Kings	22	Gen.-Ps. only	21 times
2 Kings	12		
1 Chron.	17	No more until in Isaiah	

2 Chron.	51	Isaiah	25
Ezra	10	Jeremiah	14
Nehemiah	1	Ezekiel	217
Psalms	13	Amos	21
Gen.-Psalms	212 times	Obadiah	1
		Micah	1
No more until Isaiah		Zephaniah	2
Isaiah	4	By prophets	281 times
Jeremiah	10		
Hosea	1	Total in O.T.	302 times
Amos	1		
Jonah	1		
Habakkuk	1		
By prophets	18 times		
Total in O.T.	230 times		

Adonai sold them into bondage and the dispersion. **Jehovah** will yet restore the REMNANT!

7

SEEING CHRIST IN JEHOVAH-JIREH

The Riches of His Grace (Eph. 1:7) *Manifested at Calvary!*

God is never taken by surprise. In the eternal past, the selected Lamb of God had willingly agreed that in due time He would take on human flesh and become man for the express purpose of dying for the redemption of sinful men. Divine plans are so sure that they may immediately be spoken of as if they were already done. Therefore, in God's eternal plan, Jesus Christ was "the Lamb slain from the foundation of the world," long before He was "made flesh, and dwelt among us."

Jesus fully understood what it would cost Him. He sacrificed the glories of heaven, condescended to be born in a lowly stable, was "despised and rejected of men, a man of sorrows, and acquainted with grief." Finally, stripped of all human rights, falsely condemned as an intruder and a blasphemer, He was nailed to a cross to die the infamous death of a criminal slave.

Those eternal plans, however, were progressively revealed to man over long periods of time. When Satan through the serpent seduced Adam and Eve, God promised that the Seed of the woman will yet bruise Satan's head. The first shedding of blood we read of was the animals that died to provide suitable clothing for Adam and Eve (Gen. 3:21). That, probably the first death they ever witnessed, was a dim foreshadow of the Lamb of God dying for the sins of man.

Abel's offering "of the firstlings of his flock," is the second recorded foreshadow of Christ shedding His blood for our sins. Then followed countless offerings for nearly four thousand years.

Some two thousand years after Abel, God selected Abraham to typify Himself as the Father of Him who would bruise Satan's head. He promised Abraham a son through whom that Seed would come, but withheld that reality until it was humanly impossible for Abraham or Sarah to reproduce. Sarah had been barren from her youth, and now she was also past child bearing age. Even Abraham was "now dead" (Rom. 4:19), or "as good as dead" (Heb. 11:12), as far as reproduction was concerned. Then El-Shaddai caused nature to reverse its course, because Isaac, the "Son of Promise," needed a *miracle birth* to foreshadow the Virgin Birth of Christ.

Furthermore, God chose to share with Abraham the experience of sacrificing one's only Son. First, Abraham had to give up Ishmael whom Hagar had borne to him. Ishmael was not the promised son, and because he mocked Isaac (Gen 21:9-12) he had to go. Isaac was the only son left in the home. And God said, "Take now thy son, thine only son Isaac, whom thou lovest, and get thee into the land of Moriah, and offer him there for a burnt offering, upon one of the mountains which I will tell thee of" (Gen. 22:2). (For many of the details skipped here, see chapter nineteen, *Seeing Christ Typified in Isaac.*)

Surely the question had come up before, and we have no way of knowing how it was answered. But as Abraham and Isaac ascended the mount, Isaac brought it up again: "Where is the Lamb for the burnt offering?" Abraham answered honestly, yet evasively, **"My son, God will provide himself a lamb for a burnt offering."**

Doubtlessly, there on Mount Moriah, before Abraham bound Isaac, father and son together had a warm and touching prayer meeting. They probably discussed their faith and trust in a righteous and holy God, in spite of this unusual command. Isaac by this time may have been in his early thirties (he was at least 36 when Sarah died–Gen. 23:1). He must have been willing and fully agreed to be the sacrifice. Otherwise Abraham (being a hundred years older) could not have bound him and laid him on the altar. Isaac may not have known it, but there he foreshadowed the role of Christ on Calvary.

As Abraham picked up the knife to slay his son, the Angel of Jehovah [probably Christ Himself] called unto him out of heaven, and said, "Abraham, Abraham: . . . Lay not thine hand upon the lad, neither do thou any thing unto him: for now I know that thou fearest God, seeing thou hast not withheld thy son, thine only son from me" (Gen. 22:10-12). Then and there Jehovah provided a ram, instead of Isaac, for the burnt offering (v. 13). WHAT A MESSAGE!

"And Abraham called the name of that place **Jehovah-jireh**: as it is said *to* this day, In the mount of the LORD it shall be seen"(Gen 22:14)— or *provided,* as several other versions say.

This is the only occurrence of *Jehovah-jireh* in the Bible. It is a compound name (# 3070) defined by Strong as meaning *"Jehovah will see* (to it)." We know with certainty that Jehovah, the self-existent and eternal God, did provide the One and only Lamb that could take away sin! "For it is not possible that the blood of bulls and of goats should take away sins" (Heb. 10:4). But "THIS [the blood of Jesus] is the blood of the testament which God hath enjoined unto you" (Heb. 9:20).

Imagine the joy of Abraham when the LORD intervened, and provided the ram! Jesus could well say, "Abraham rejoiced to see my day : and he saw it, and was glad" (John 8:56).

This event emphasizes two very vital truths. *First,* although Abraham was a godly man of faith, and Isaac was a faithful son, even *the son of promise,* sacrificing Isaac could not have saved one soul—not even his own! *Second,* Isaac at that moment needed a substitute. The ram served that purpose well, *temporarily.*

But Isaac, like all of us, eventually needed more than a substitute. A substitute is something that replaces the genuine, and can again be replaced by another. The ram was only a substitute, but Jesus is the GENUINE which can never be replaced by any other. That's the bottom line of JEHOVAH-JIREH! **The LORD has seen to it, and provided.**

8

SEEING CHRIST IN JEHOVAH-ROPHE

"The LORD that healeth thee" (Ex. 15:26c)

This was the first name of God introduced to Israel after their deliverance from Egypt. All the basic names already discussed were used in the Genesis account. Even His name Jehovah (translated LORD or GOD, all capital letters) occurs 163 times in Genesis. And God had not yet made Himself [fully] known to them by that name (Ex. 6:3). There are yet seven more Hebrew names compounded with Jehovah, which we want to consider.

I marvel at how these names progressively reveal the multiple aspects of Christ. These new names are no greater nor more important than those already studied, but each one adds some new dimension to our understanding of our Savior, Lord, and King.

We can hardly comprehend the joy of Israel after having crossed the Red Sea on dry ground, while their pursuing enemies were consumed by the sea. Thirteen times they applauded the name **Jehovah** (the God of Revelation and Redemption) in their song of victory (Ex. 15:1-21).

Nor can we comprehend the intense trial that immediately followed. For three days they traveled, "and found no water" (v. 22). That is worse than three days without food. Then they came to Marah and found water—but "they could not drink of the waters of Marah, for they were bitter" (v. 23).

Bitter waters typify death without Christ. The third trumpet judgment includes bitter waters, wreaking death on Christless souls (Rev. 8:11).

In Israel's distress Moses cried unto the LORD, who showed him a tree that would sweeten the waters. That tree (whatever it was) typified Jesus Christ, the Tree of Life. To cast a tree into the water, it had to be cut. Cutting the tree foreshadowed Jesus' death, "for he was cut off out of the land of the living: for the transgression of my people was he stricken" (Isa. 53:8b). That tree, by contact, sweetened the waters of Marah. **Death is sweet when Christ is in it.**

> "There he made for them a statute and an ordinance, and there he proved them, and said, If thou wilt diligently hearken to the voice of the LORD thy God, and wilt do that which is right in his sight, and wilt give ear to his commandments, and keep all his statutes, I will put none of these diseases upon thee, which I have brought upon the Egyptians: **for I *am* the LORD that healeth thee**"(Ex.15:25b, 26).

The combination *Jehovah-rophe* is found only once, but the promise and incidents of healing occur frequently in the Old and New Testaments. All healing comes from God, whether physical, emotional, mental or spiritual. Sometimes He uses natural means, and sometimes supernatural.

Following are a few Old Testament examples demonstrating a variety of His healing powers:

- Healing barren women: Sarah and Rebekah (Gen. 18:9-14; 25:21)
- Healing for bitter water at Jericho (2 Kings 2:19-22)
- Healing for King Hezekiah (2 Kings 20:1-7)
- Healing for their land (2 Chron. 7:14)
- Healing for all thy diseases (Ps. 103:3)
- Healing for the broken in heart (Ps. 147:3)
- Healing for your backslidings (Jer. 3:22; Hos. 14:4).

The New Testament shows that the **Great Physician is Jesus Christ Himself.** He healed all manner of sickness, physical and spiritual:

- He healed all manner of sickness (Mt. 4:23-24)
- He healed several lepers (Mt. 8:1-4)
- He healed the centurion's servant (Mt. 8:5-13)
- He healed Peter's mother-in-law (Mt. 8:14-15)
- He healed many possessed with devils (Mt. 8:16-17)
- He healed demoniacs exceedingly fierce (Mt. 8:28-33)
- He healed a man sick of the palsy (Mt. 9:1-8; Mk. 2:3-12)
- He healed the woman with an issue of blood (Mt. 9:20-22)
- He healed two blind men that followed Him (Mt. 9:27-31)
- He healed the withered hand (Mt. 12:10-13)
- He healed one blind and speechless (Mt. 12:22-30)
- He healed perfectly all that touched Him (Mt. 14:34-36)
- He healed a sorely vexed lunatic (Mt. 17:14-21)
- He healed blind men by the wayside (Mt. 20:30-34)
- He healed a man with an unclean spirit (Mk. 1:23-26)
- He healed all that had divers diseases (Lu. 4:40)
- He healed many possessed with devils (Lu. 4:41)
- He healed a woman's infirmity of 18 years (Lu. 13:11-17)
- He healed ten lepers in one act (Lu. 17:11-19)
- He healed the nobleman's son (John 4:46-54)
- He healed a man blind from birth (Jn. 9:1-7)

I'm sure this is not a complete list of His healings, but it is enough to show that **Jesus Christ is our Jehovah-Rophe. He is the only remedy for sin—"the LORD that healeth thee."**

9

SEEING CHRIST IN JEHOVAH-NISSI

The LORD our Banner (Ex. 17:15)

Israel had just arrived at Horeb and again were desperately in need of water. This time God said,

> "Behold, I will stand before thee there upon the rock in Horeb; and thou shalt smite the rock, and there shall come water out of it, that the people may drink. And Moses did so in the sight of the elders of Israel" (Ex. 17:6).

There was an abundant flow of fresh, clean water. Flowing water typifies the Holy Spirit. The smitten Rock, from which the water flowed, foreshadowed Christ smitten and dying for our sins. Sometime in the eternal past Christ had committed Himself to become the atoning sacrifice for fallen man. He was already sustaining Israel spiritually, "for they drank of that spiritual Rock that followed them: **and that Rock was Christ**" (1 Cor. 10:4).

"Then came Amalek, and fought with Israel in Rephidim" (Ex. 17:8). Amalek was a grandson of Esau (Gen. 36:12) who, when seeing the pottage Jacob had prepared for himself, willingly bartered his birthright for one meal. "Thus Esau despised his birthright" (25:29-34). He lived for immediate self-gratification. Later "he found no place for repentance, though he sought it carefully with tears" (Heb. 12:16, 17). He was not seeking repentance from sin; he was only seeking to reverse the consequences of the bad deal he had made by despising his birthright (Gen. 25:32).

Amalek was even worse than Esau. He was possessed with a fighting spirit. When he saw Israel enjoying water from the Rock in Horeb, he made war with them to rob them of that treasure. Near the end of Moses' life he wrote a brief account of that attack:

> "Remember what Amalek did unto thee by the way, when ye were come forth out of Egypt; how he met thee by the way, and smote the hindmost of thee, *even* all *that were* feeble behind thee, when thou *wast* faint and weary; and **he feared not God**" (Dt. 25:17-18).

Thus Amalek typifies our own natural (*unregenerated*) man. When a Christan is born again, he receives the Holy Spirit. "He is a new creature: old things are passed away; behold, all things are become new" (2 Cor. 5:17). But there will be conflict, because our carnal flesh will not fear God, nor submit willingly to the Holy Spirit. Only by the power of **Jehovah-nissi** will we be able to bring our carnal nature under control.

Amalek "was the first of the nations [to attack Israel— thus he also typifies the world system]; but his latter end shall be that he perish for ever" (Nu. 24:20). Our *natural man* and the *world system* wage perpetual warfare against the new man in Christ. As long as we live here in this life we need to do like Paul did. "But I discipline my body and bring it into subjection, lest, when I have preached to others, I myself should become disqualified" (1 Cor. 9:27, NKJ).

At Amalek's attack was the first time that Israel was called upon to do battle. In their conflicts with Pharaoh, and when the Red Sea blocked their passage, or when they were in distress for water, God always did everything for them. But with Amalek (typifying our natural man) Israel is requested to do battle. And unless Moses' hands were lifted up [in prayer to God], Amalek prevailed (Ex. 17:11).

"And the LORD said unto Moses, Write this *for* a memorial in a book, and rehearse *it* in the ears of Joshua: for I will utterly put out the remembrance of Amalek from under heaven. . . . For he said, Because the LORD hath sworn that the LORD will have war with Amalek from generation to generation" (Ex. 17:14, 16).

"Therefore it shall be, when the LORD thy God hath given thee rest from all thine enemies round about, in the land which the LORD thy God giveth thee for an inheritance to possess it, that thou shalt blot out the remembrance of Amalek from under heaven; **thou shalt not forget it**" (Dt. 25:19).

After Amalek was defeated, "Moses built an altar, and called the name of it **Jehovah-nissi** [the LORD our Banner]" (Ex. 17:15). A banner is the emblem (such as a national flag) by which an army is identified. It represents and designates the political powers behind that army. *Jehovah-nissi* designates our **Jehovah God** as the spiritual Power we need to control and conquer our fallen nature.

God did not exterminate Amalek, just like He does not eradicate a Christian's flesh. But He **commands us** to mortify [put to death] the deeds of the body **through the Spirit** (Rom. 8:13; Col. 3:5).

Later, King Saul was commanded to destroy Amalek. The instructions were explicit:

"Thus saith the LORD of hosts, I remember *that* which Amalek did to Israel, how he laid *wait* for him in the way, when he came up from Egypt. Now go and smite Amalek, and utterly destroy all that they have, and spare them not; but slay both man and woman, infant and suckling, ox and sheep, camel and ass" (1 Sam. 15:2-3).

God gave him victory over the Amalekites, and provided everything he needed to complete the task. But Saul deliberately stopped short of what God had told him to do. (If Saul had completed his assignment there would have been no Haman to seek the Jews' destruction in the time of Esther.) God equips the Christian with the grace to crucify the self-life, but He expects us to participate in the crucifixion. We must reckon ourselves "to be dead indeed unto sin, but alive unto God through Jesus Christ our Lord" (Rom. 6:11).

God can never make peace with our natural man (*carnal nature*), because "flesh and blood cannot inherit the kingdom of God" (1 Cor. 15:50). Therefore we "**must** be born again." With Christ as our Captain, Lord, and King, and by the power of the Holy Spirit within, we are requested to keep our body under, "and bring it into subjection" (1 Cor. 9:27). But we in our own strength cannot conquer our carnal nature, the flesh. We **must** align ourselves as Christian soldiers under the banner of Jesus Christ, **our Jehovah-nissi.** In Him there is victory.

10

SEEING CHRIST IN JEHOVAH-M'KADDESH
The LORD that Sanctifies (Lev. 20:8)

"**Sanctify yourselves** therefore, and be holy: for I *am* the LORD your God. And you shall keep My statutes, and perform them: I *am* the LORD which sanctifies you" (Lev 20:7-8, NKJV).

Sanctification requires our willingness, submission, and cooperation. We cannot do it alone, and God **will not** sanctify an unwilling, unsubmissive, uncooperative rebel.

Jehovah-M'Kaddesh is not transliterated in our English versions, nor identified by capitalization like the name Jehovah, but He **sanctifies** those who commit themselves to Him (Lev. 20:8; 21:8, 15, 23; 22:9, 16). He cleanses from sin, makes holy, and sets apart for holy purposes.

First, He sanctified (set apart) a day of rest, for worship (Gen. 2:3). Next, He instructed Moses, "Sanctify unto me all the firstborn, . . . of man and of beast: it is mine" (Ex. 13:2). Their firstborn had been spared from death by properly applying the blood (Ex. 12:12, 13). That blood foreshadowed the blood of Christ, without which no one can be sanctified or saved.

Without faith in the Blood of Christ neither Israel nor any of us could be saved, sanctified, or made holy. He commands us, "Be ye holy, for I am holy." That means we must do our part (rightly believe in Christ, confess, repent, willingly submit, respond, and receive). I repeat, He will not sanctify any of us without our **willingness, submission, and cooperation**. He does not make puppets of anyone!

That **Christ** is our means unto sanctification is evident in His High Priestly prayer:

> "They are not of the world, even as I am not of the world. **Sanctify** them through thy truth: thy word is truth. As thou hast sent me into the world, even so have I also sent them into the world. And for their sakes I **sanctify** myself, that they also might be **sanctified** through the truth" (John 17:16-19).

Other scriptures show that **sanctification requires cleansing and holiness:**

> "Know ye not that the unrighteous shall not inherit the kingdom of God? Be not deceived: neither fornicators, nor idolaters, nor adulterers, nor effeminate, nor abusers of themselves with mankind, nor thieves, nor covetous, nor drunkards, nor revilers, nor extortioners, shall inherit the kingdom of God. And such were some of you: but ye are **washed**, but ye are **sanctified**, but ye are **justified** in the name of the **Lord Jesus**, and by the Spirit of our God" (1 Cor 6:9-11).

> "For this is the will of God, *even* your **sanctification**, that ye should abstain from fornication: that every one of you should know how to possess his vessel in **sanctification** and honour; not in the lust of concupiscence, even as the Gentiles which know not God: . . . For God hath not called us unto uncleanness, but unto **holiness**" (1 Thess 4:3-5, 7).

Sanctification and holiness are available to us only through the atoning blood of Jesus Christ. He is indeed **our Jehovah-M'Kaddesh**—"the LORD who sanctifies you" (Lev. 20:8, NKJV).

Enroute from Egypt to the Promised Land the LORD presented Himself as **Jehovah-rophe**— the Great Physician who offers healing for spirit, soul, and body; **Jehovah-nissi**—the Captain who offers strength for spiritual victory; and **Jehovah-M'Kaddesh**—the Sanctifier who sets apart for holy purposes. Christ is all of that to us, and more.

11

SEEING CHRIST IN JEHOVAH-SHALOM

Jehovah [is our] Peace (Judg. 6:24)

Joshua and all his contemporaries had died. "There arose another generation after them, which knew not the LORD." Israel plunged into idolatry, and peace departed from them. Judges 1:19-34 lists eight instances where Israel had failed to drive out those idolatrous nations as God had commanded them.

> "And an angel of the LORD came up from Gilgal to Bochim, and said, I made you to go up out of Egypt, and have brought you unto the land which I sware unto your fathers; and I said, I will never break my covenant with you. And ye shall make no league with the inhabitants of this land; ye shall throw down their altars: but ye have not obeyed my voice: why have ye done this? Wherefore I also said, I will not drive them out from before you; but they shall be *as thorns* in your sides, and their gods shall be a snare unto you" (Judges 2:1-3).

Judges six reports the fourth of the seven cycles of apostasy in the Book of Judges. At that time the LORD had delivered Israel into the hand of Midian.

> "And the hand of Midian prevailed against Israel: *and* because of the Midianites the children of Israel made them the dens which *are* in the mountains, and caves, and strong holds. And *so* it was, when Israel had sown, that the Midianites came up, and the Amalekites, and the children of the east, even they

came up against them; and they encamped against them, and
destroyed the increase of the earth, till thou come unto Gaza, and
left no sustenance for Israel, neither sheep, nor ox, nor ass. For
they came up with their cattle and their tents, and they came as
grasshoppers for multitude; *for* both they and their camels were
without number: and they entered into the land to destroy it. And
Israel was greatly impoverished because of the Midianites; and
the children of Israel cried unto the LORD" (Judges 6:2-6).

God, in His mercy, heard their cry and sent an angel of the
LORD who commissioned Gideon to deliver Israel. Study
carefully verses 11-23, especially verses 12, 14, 16, 21-23.
By comparing these verses with Exodus 23:20-23; 33:14 and
Isaiah 63:9, I am persuaded that this was indeed **the Angel of
the LORD**—our pre-incarnate Jehovah—Christ Himself.

(I commend the *New King James, The New Jerusalem
Bible*, and *The Berkeley Version* for having capitalized Angel
in this passage. The Bible is our best commentary available
on such matters.)

"Gideon said, Alas, O Lord **GOD** [Adonai **Jehovah**]! for
because I have seen an angel of the LORD face to face. And the
LORD said unto him, **Peace** **be** **unto thee**; fear not: thou shalt
not die. Then Gideon built an altar there unto the LORD, and
called it **Jehovah-shalom**" (6:22b-24a).

Gideon recognized our **LORD Jehovah** as the true peace
of Israel. Therefore he named his altar **Jehovah-shalom
(Jehovah is Peace).**

"And it came to pass the same night, that the LORD said
unto him, Take thy father's young bullock, even the second bullock of seven years old, and throw down the altar of Baal that thy
father hath, and cut down the grove that *is* by it: And build an
altar unto the LORD thy God upon the top of this rock, in the
ordered place, and take the second bullock, and offer a burnt sacrifice with the wood of the grove which thou shalt cut down.
Then Gideon took ten men of his servants, and did as the LORD
had said unto him: and *so* it was, because he feared his father's
household, and the men of the city, that he could not do *it* by day,
that he did *it* by night" (Judges 6:25-27).

Having received a double confirmation by the fleece he had laid (Judges 6:36-40), Gideon was assured of victory over the hordes of Midianites and Amalekites that encamped against them. When God said his army was too big, and reduced it from 32,000 to three hundred men (7:2-8), his faith did not waver. Instead of weapons, God chose lamps, broken pitchers and trumpets to deliver Israel (7:1-25).

> "Thus was Midian subdued before the children of Israel, so that they lifted up their heads no more. And the country was in quietness forty years in the days of Gideon" (Judges 8:28).

Their quietness and peace were vouchsafed in their **Jehovah-shalom.** It was a physical foreshadow in Israel of the spiritual peace even Gentiles can have in Christ Jesus.

> "But now **in Christ Jesus** ye who sometimes were far off are made nigh by the blood of Christ. **For he is our peace [our JEHOVAH-SHALOM],** who hath made both one, and hath broken down the middle wall of partition *between us;* having abolished in his flesh the enmity, ... for to make in himself of twain one new man, *so* **making peace**" (Eph 2:13-15).

12
SEEING CHRIST IN JEHOVAH-ROHI

The LORD is my Shepherd (Psalm 23:1).

As King David, perhaps in his latter years, reminisced about his walk with the Lord, he must have recalled that God was always there when he needed Him, and always sufficient for every need! As a boy, when he was feeding his father's sheep, "there came a lion, and a bear, and took a lamb out of the flock." Each time he was impelled by a shepherd's heart and by faith in God to rescue that lamb. God was with him and enabled him to kill both the lion and the bear.

Later, while King Saul saw him as a mere "stripling," he approached Goliath armed only with a sling and five stones. By faith he saw more of God than he did of Goliath, and he knew that Goliath was no match for God. With full assurance he said to Goliath:

> "Thou comest to me with a sword, and with a spear, and with a shield: but I come to thee in the name of the LORD of hosts, the God of the armies of Israel, whom thou hast defied. This day will the LORD deliver thee into mine hand; and I will smite thee, and take thine head from thee; and I will give the carcases of the host of the Philistines this day unto the fowls of the air, and to the wild beasts of the earth; that all the earth may know that there is a God in Israel. And all this assembly shall know that the LORD saveth not with sword and spear: for the battle *is* the LORD'S, and he will give you into our hands" (1 Sam 17:45-47).

Still later, when King Saul with an army of 3,000 men, sought David's life, the same God was still with David and always delivered him.   When the Amalekites had burned Ziklag and taken all the people captive, including David's wives, he and his men "wept until they had no more power to weep. . . .   And David was greatly distressed; for the people spake of stoning him, . . . but David encouraged himself in the LORD" (1 Sam. 30:4, 6). And the LORD gave them grace to overtake the Amalekites, to recover everything, and to gain much spoil.

God was always present, much more so than those Eastern shepherds who virtually lived with their sheep day and night. They knew each sheep by name and knew its characteristics. Much more, God knows each of His sheep better than we know ourselves.

Therefore with deep feeling David exclaimed, "The LORD is my **shepherd**." To David that meant He lives with me day and night. He knows not only my every act, but my every need, my every ailment, thought, feeling, and every lack of feeling. He knew that with the LORD as his Shepherd he would never be in want of proper care.

David, by experience, knew very well the role of a shepherd. A phrase by phrase and word by word analysis of Psalm 23 gives an excellent description of the LORD as a divine Shepherd.

> "The LORD *is* my shepherd; I shall not want. He maketh me to lie down in green pastures: he leadeth me beside the still waters. He restoreth my soul: he leadeth me in the paths of righteousness for his name's sake.
>
> "Yea, though I walk through the valley of the shadow of death, I will fear no evil: for thou *art* with me; thy rod and thy staff they comfort me. Thou preparest a table before me in the presence of mine enemies: thou anointest my head with oil; my cup runneth over.
>
> "Surely goodness and mercy shall follow me all the days of my life: and I will dwell in the house of the LORD for ever" (Psa. 23:1-6).

David knew the LORD to be all-sufficient for every need in this life and **for ever.**

Isaiah prophesied of the coming of Jesus Christ, saying,

> "Behold, the Lord GOD [Adonai Jehovah] will come with strong *hand,* and his arm shall rule for him: behold, his reward *is* with him, and his work before him. He shall feed his flock **like a shepherd:** he shall gather the lambs with his arm, and carry *them* in his bosom, *and* shall gently lead those that are with young" (Isa 40:10-11).

Jesus said, "I am the **good shepherd:** the **good shepherd** giveth his life for the sheep" (John 10:11). "I am the good shepherd, and know my sheep, and am known of mine" (v. 14).

> "For ye were as sheep going astray; but are now returned unto the Shepherd and Bishop of your souls" (1 Peter 2:25).

> "Now the God of peace, that brought again from the dead our Lord Jesus, **that great shepherd** of the sheep, through the blood of the everlasting covenant, make you perfect in every good work to do his will, working in you that which is wellpleasing in his sight, **through Jesus Christ [our Jehovah-Rohi];** to whom *be* glory for ever and ever. Amen" (Heb 13:20, 21).

13

SEEING CHRIST IN JEHOVAH-TSIDKENUE

Jehovah our Righteousness (Jer. 23:6b)

Jehovah-tsidkenue is the name by which the LORD revealed Himself through Jeremiah. The Northern Kingdom had fallen more than a hundred years before this was written. Many from Judah were already carried to Babylon, and Jerusalem's doom was already pronounced. We will let THE LORD OUR RIGHTEOUSNESS tell us what He is going to do with His chosen people, now battered, shattered, and scattered.

"And I will gather the remnant of my flock out of all countries whither I have driven them, and will bring them again to their folds; and they shall be fruitful and increase. And I will set up shepherds over them which shall feed them: and they shall fear no more, nor be dismayed, neither shall they be lacking, saith the LORD.

"**Behold, the days come, saith the LORD,** that I will raise unto David a **righteous Branch,** and **a King shall reign** and prosper, and shall execute judgment and justice in the earth. In his days **Judah** shall be saved, and **Israel** shall dwell safely: **and this *is* his name whereby he shall be called, THE LORD OUR RIGHTEOUSNESS.**

"Therefore, **behold, the days come, saith the LORD,** that they shall no more say, The LORD liveth, which brought up the children of Israel out of the land of Egypt; but, The LORD liveth, which brought up and which led the seed of the house of Israel out of the north country, and from all countries whither I had driven them; and they shall dwell in their own land" (Jer. 23:3-8).

"Behold, **the days come,** saith the LORD, that I will perform that good thing which I have promised unto the house of Israel and to the house of Judah. In those days, and at that time, will I cause the Branch of righteousness to grow up unto David; and he shall execute judgment and righteousness in the land. In those days shall Judah be saved, and Jerusalem shall dwell safely: and this *is the name* wherewith **she** shall be called, **The LORD our righteousness"** (Jer. 33:14-16).

"In those days, and in that time, saith the LORD, the children of Israel shall come, they and the children of Judah together, going and weeping: they shall go, and seek the LORD their God. They shall ask the way to Zion with their faces thitherward, *saying,* Come, and let us join ourselves to the LORD in a perpetual covenant *that* shall not be forgotten" (Jer. 50:4-5).

"And I will bring Israel again to his habitation, and he shall feed on Carmel and Bashan, and his soul shall be satisfied upon mount Ephraim and Gilead. In those days, and in that time, saith the LORD, the iniquity of Israel shall be sought for, and *there shall be* none; and the sins of Judah, and they shall not be found: for I will pardon them whom I reserve" (Jer. 50:19-20).

The phrase, *"behold, the days come,"* occurs fifteen times in Jeremiah alone: three times foretelling Israel's punishment (7:32; 9:25; 19:6); eight times, their restoration (16:14-15; 23:5, 7; 30:3; 31:27, 31, 38; 33:14); four times, judgment upon their enemies. Jeremiah, the weeping prophet, sorrowed intensely for the spiritual sins and the national collapse of his people Israel. But he also saw, by divine inspiration, some of the cleansing, redeeming, and restoring power of **Jehovah-tsidkenue**—the LORD our RIGHTEOUSNESS.

14
SEEING CHRIST IN JEHOVAH-SHAMMAH

"The LORD is there" (Ezek. 48:35b).

The revelation which Ezekiel describes in chapters 40-48, came to him in the twenty-fifth year of his captivity in Babylon (40:1), fourteen years after the fall of Jerusalem. While we may have varied views on these chapters, I trust we all agree that the Lord had brought Ezekiel *in the visions of God* into the land of Israel (Ezek. 40:1, 2), and showed him things that we do not fully understand. Among them are the precise measurements of the temple which he described, and of the land surrounding it. Some things we need to accept with reverence and with silence.

> "And he said unto me, Son of man, the place of my throne, and the place of the soles of my feet, where I will dwell in the midst of the children of Israel for ever, and my holy name, shall the house of Israel no more defile, *neither* they, nor their kings, by their whoredom, nor by the carcases of their kings in their high places" (Ezek 43:7).

John the Revelator also describes a city that surpasses our comprehension:

> "And I saw a new heaven and a new earth: for the first heaven and the first earth were passed away; and there was no more sea. And I John saw the holy city, new Jerusalem, coming down from God out of heaven, prepared as a bride adorned for her husband. And I heard a great voice out of heaven saying, Behold,

the tabernacle of God *is* with men, and he will dwell with them, and they shall be his people, and God himself shall be with them, *and be* their God" (Rev. 21:1-3).

"The secret things belong unto the Lord our God: but those things which are revealed belong unto us and to our children for ever, that we may do . . . [what He asks of us]" (Dt. 29:29).   We let the unknown rest with the Lord, but we accept without question that "the name of the city from that day shall be, **The LORD is There**" (Ezek. 48:35b), emphasizing the **PERSONAL   PRESENCE of our Lord Jesus Christ** .

The Christian's Jehovah-shammah is "CHRIST in you, the hope of glory" (Col. 1:27).

CONCLUSION

What impresses me most of all in considering the many Hebrew names of God revealed in the Old Testament, is that every name includes our Lord Jesus Christ, and that Christ is the New Testament fulfillment of every one.   If we study deeply and sincerely, we are bound to **see glimpses of Christ in the Old Testament** (hundreds of them), and their **glorious fulfillment in the New Testament.**

"For unto us a child is born, unto us a son is given: and the government shall be upon his shoulder: and his name shall be called Wonderful, Counsellor, The mighty God, The everlasting Father, The Prince of Peace. Of the increase of *his* government and peace *there shall be* no end, upon the throne of David, and upon his kingdom, to order it, and to establish it with judgment and with justice from henceforth even for ever. The zeal of the LORD of hosts will perform this" (Isa 9:6-7) .

Part III

Seeing Christ Typified
in
Bible Characters

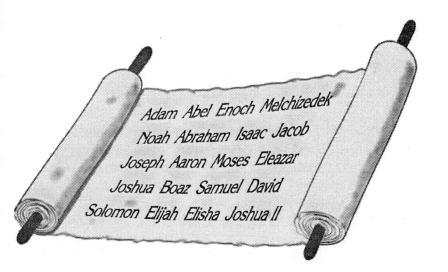

Adam Abel Enoch Melchizedek
Noah Abraham Isaac Jacob
Joseph Aaron Moses Eleazar
Joshua Boaz Samuel David
Solomon Elijah Elisha Joshua II

15

SEEING CHRIST TYPIFIED IN ADAM AND ABEL

Glimpses of His pre-incarnate glory which He had
with the Father before the world was. John 17:5

I. SEEING CHRIST TYPIFIED IN ADAM

"God created man in his *own* image, in the image of God
created he him; male and female created he them. And God
blessed them, and God said unto them, Be fruitful, and multiply,
and replenish the earth, and subdue it: and have dominion over
the fish of the sea, and over the fowl of the air, and over every
living thing that moveth upon the earth" (Gen. 1:27-28).

"And the LORD God formed man *of* the dust of the ground,
and breathed into his nostrils the breath of life; and man became
a living soul" (Gen. 2:7).

When the LORD God (Jehovah Elohim) breathed into
Adam's nostrils the breath of life, Adam sprang to life, a *living soul*. As a threefold being, consisting of spirit, soul, and
body, he represented the Holy Trinity. Created in the image
of God, and given dominion over every living thing that
moveth on the earth, in the sea, and in the air, he dimly foreshadowed Christ. For Christ is the **express image** of God, the
brightness of His glory, and upholds all things by the word of
His power (Heb. 1:2, 3)! The *Substance* is always superior to
the *shadow*.

Fresh from the hand of God Adam was perfect, pure, holy, righteous, and flawless ("the figure of HIM that was to come," Rom. 5:14).   He was thoroughly educated, well equipped with a language, and an intelligence that has not been matched, *except by Christ,* since the fall of man. Otherwise he could not have named "every beast of the field and every fowl of the air" on the first day of his life!

> "And the LORD God caused a deep sleep to fall upon Adam, and he slept: and he took one of his ribs, and closed up the flesh instead thereof; and the rib, which the LORD God had taken from man, made he a woman, and brought her unto the man. And Adam said, This *is* now bone of my bones, and flesh of my flesh: she shall be called Woman, because she was taken out of Man" (Gen. 2:21-23).

Adam's *deep sleep* foreshadowed Christ's death on the cross. Taking a rib out of his side to *build* [1] a wife for Adam typified the pierced side of Christ from which flowed the blood (John 19:34) for the purchase of His Bride, the church (Acts 20:28). Paul shows the figurative meaning of Adam's *"bone of my bones, and flesh of my flesh."* "For we are members of [Christ's] body, of his flesh and of his bones. . . . This is a great mystery: but I speak concerning Christ and the church" (Eph. 5:30, 32). Adam and Eve typified Christ and the church in several ways.

As Adam is the fountain head of everyone born into the human race, so Christ is the spiritual Head of the church— which includes every **born again** believer in Christ. The Old Testament "is the book of the generations [plural] of Adam" (Gen. 5:1). The New Testament is "the book of the generation [singular–*there are no grandchildren*] of Jesus Christ" (Mt. 1:1).

---

[1] The King James Version says God *made* a woman from Adam's rib. Both the Hebrew and Luther's German translation say He *built* a woman. Eve typifies the church; and the church is not created, but built. Jesus said, "Upon this rock I will *build* my church" (Mt. 16:18).

Before his Fall, Adam typified Christ primarily by similarities, but typology is not confined to similarities. After the Fall, Adam typified Christ mostly by contrasts. "For as **in Adam all die**, even so **in Christ shall all be made alive**" (1 Cor. 15:22).

> "And so it is written, The **first man Adam was made a living soul**; the **last Adam** *was made* a **quickening [i.e. life-giving] spirit.** Howbeit that *was* not first which is spiritual, but that which is natural; and afterward that which is spiritual. **The first man** *is* **of the earth, earthy: the second man** *is* **the Lord from heaven.** As *is* the earthy, such *are* they also that are earthy: and as *is* the heavenly, such *are* they also that are heavenly. And **as we have borne the image of the earthy, we shall also bear the image of the heavenly**" (1 Cor 15:45-49).

The above references along with Romans 5:12-21 give us a list of contrasts between two one-man activities. Setting them in two columns (Adam in the first column, Christ in the second column) will help to amplify the contrasts.

Adam was made a living soul	Christ was made a life-giving Spirit
In Adam all die	All in Christ are made alive
First man is of the earth, earthy	Second Man, the Lord from heaven
We've borne the earthy image	We shall bear the heavenly image
By one man sin entered	By one Man sin is taken away
Death passed upon all men	Life is restored to all true believers
By the Law sin is imputed	By faith in Christ sin is excluded
By Adam's sin death reigned	By salvation in Christ grace reigns
By one offense many be dead	In Christ grace abounds unto many
Violation unto condemnation	Sinners cleansed unto justification
By one man death reigned	By one Man righteousness reigns
Judgment came upon all men	Righteousness unto justification
One disobedience, all sinners	Obedience of One, many righteous
Law entered, sin revealed	Grace abounded, sin repealed
Sin reigns unto death	Grace reigns through righteousness

"Wherefore the law was our schoolmaster [disciplinarian, so the German] to bring us unto Christ, that we might be justified by faith. But after that faith is come, we are no longer under a schoolmaster. For we are all the children of God by faith in Christ Jesus" (Gal. 3:24-26).

"Which were born, not of blood, nor of the will of the flesh, nor of the will of man, but of God" (John 1:13). As Adam and the Old Testament represent our first birth, so Christ and the New Testament represent our second birth. WE MUST BE BORN AGAIN.

II. SEEING CHRIST TYPIFIED IN ABEL

The life of Abel was short, but of worthy significance. Being the second birth in the human race, he seems to typify the *second birth* of all who are born again. Born of fallen parents he inherited their fallen nature. This he acknowledged by bringing to the LORD an acceptable sacrifice (Gen. 4:4). But there is no record of any sin or misdeeds in his life. Although he had a fallen nature, he must have kept it under control by faith, which God expects of all born again Christians. Since the Holy Spirit was not yet given, Abel could not have had an actual new birth, but his faith, his life, and his death were a beautiful foreshadow of born again Christianity.

Paul, in contrasting Adam with Christ, said , "The first man is of the earth, earthy: the second man is the Lord from heaven." Can we not, in a figure, apply part of that statement to Cain and Abel? That Cain was very *earthy* is abundantly evident. Abel was not the Lord from heaven, but his "more excellent sacrifice" which he offered by faith (Heb. 11:4), as well as his life and death appear like a foreshadow of the life and death of Christ.

Jesus spoke of "all the *righteous blood* shed upon the earth, . . . [including] the blood of *righteous Abel*" (Mt. 23:35). The Hebrew writer uses Abel's blood in contrast to Christ's blood, "that speaketh better things than that of Abel" (12:24). John testifies that Abel was slain because of his righteous works (1 John 3:12). The shadow (Abel) bears witness to the Substance (Christ).

One thing, however, we dare not overlook. While Abel was an innocent and a righteous man, the shedding of his blood could not save one soul! The voice of his blood cried unto God out of the ground (Gen. 4:10), but guilt, guilt, guilt, was all it could say. Only the blood of Christ can offer pardon and peace to those who receive Him!

Abel is set before us as a proper *example*, but Christ is set forth to be *the propitiation* for sins. Abel offered to God a lamb as an atonement for his own sins, but Christ offered Himself as the Lamb of God for our sins. "Neither is there salvation in any other: for there is none other name under heaven given among men, whereby we must be saved."

16

SEEING CHRIST TYPIFIED IN ENOCH

Typifying Christ in the flesh walking with God,
then ascending up into heaven.

"And Enoch lived sixty and five years, and begat Methuselah: And **Enoch walked with God** after he begat Methuselah three hundred years, and begat sons and daughters: And all the days of Enoch were three hundred sixty and five years: And **Enoch walked with God**: and he *was* not; for God took him" (Gen 5:21-24).

What a brief biography. What a powerful testimony! Of only two men does the Bible say they "walked with God." It is said once of Noah (Gen. 6:9); twice of Enoch. "Can two walk together, except they be agreed" (Amos 3:3)? Enoch agreed with God, and God was pleased with Enoch.

Enoch was the seventh generation of the human race, in the Sethite line—those who "began to call upon the name of the LORD" (Gen. 4:26). (*Seven,* in Biblical numerology, is often called the number of perfection. It must be a very important number, occurring 463 times in the Bible; *seventh,* 120 times; *seventy,* 61 times; for a total of 644 times.)

Enoch had no Bible, no Bible concordance, and no Bible dictionary. But he knew God. He had developed a personal relationship with God by walking with Him. He communed with God, agreed with Him, and fully trusted Him. Otherwise he could not have "pleased God," as the Bible testifies of him.

"By faith Enoch was translated that he should not see death; and was not found, because God had translated him: for before his translation he had this testimony, that **he pleased God**" (Heb. 11:5).

Without faith it is impossible to please God (Heb. 11:6). Hereby we know that Enoch was a man of faith. He walked with God by faith. When Enoch was sixty-five years old he begat Methuselah, after which "he walked with God . . . three hundred years, and begat sons and daughters." Evidently the birth of a son intensified his intimacy with, and his reliance upon, God.

Enoch walking in close fellowship with God here on earth foreshadows Christ Incarnate, walking daily in even closer fellowship with His Father. Jesus in His character reflected "the brightness of [the Father's] glory, and the express image of His person." Therefore He could truly say, "He that hath seen me hath seen the Father" (John 14:9).

As the first man to be taken up without dying, Enoch typifies two important events. First, it typifies the Ascension of Jesus Christ from the Mount of Olives (Acts 1:9-11). Jesus, however, had died and risen again. "Death hath no more dominion over him" (Rom. 6:9)—nor over Enoch.

Second, it foreshadows a *great separation*!

Enoch thus taken up typifies the redeemed who "are alive and remain unto the coming of the Lord . . ., [who] shall be caught up [*harpadzo*, # *726*] . . . to meet the Lord in the air" (1 Thess. 4:15-17). It will be a separation. "One shall be taken [*paralambano* # *3880*] and the other left [*aphieemi* # *863*]" (Mt. 24:40, 41; Luke 17:34, 35, 36).

Taken and *left* are opposites in these verses. *Taken* is from the same word that Jesus used when He said, "I will come again, and *receive* [*paralambano*] you unto myself; that where I am, there ye may be also" (John 14:3). The angel used the same word when he said to Joseph of Nazareth, "Fear not to *take unto thee* [*paralambano*] Mary thy wife"

(Mt. 1:20b). *Left* means forsaken. Example, "Then all the disciples *forsook* [*aphieemi*] him, and fled" (Mt. 26:56b).

The word *took* (*airo # 142*, Mt. 24:39) is not synonymous with *paralambano* (24:40, 41). *Airo* means to *remove, take away*. Example: "Bind him hand and foot, and *take* him *away*" (Mt. 22:13a). *Paralambano* means taken along side, like a wife; *airo* means taken out of the way.

When Enoch was taken he broke the "he died" monotony (Gen. 5:5-19) with a ray of hope and a spark of life. For six generations they all died. Physical death is a usual gateway to eternal life. But in Enoch the Lord chose to give us a beautiful foreshadow of **Life without dying**. One of these times, most surely in (if *not before*) the **seventh** millennium, all true Christians will take the *Enoch route* to heaven, the route that Jesus took when He ascended from the Mount of Olives (Acts 1:9-11).

"Even so, Come, Lord Jesus." Let's not miss it!

17

SEEING CHRIST TYPIFIED IN

NOAH AND THE ARK

Glimpses of His pre-incarnate Glory which He had
with the Father before the world was. John 17:5

Noah was the tenth generation of mankind. Already the
human race was so corrupt that God saw it best to cleanse the
world with a universal flood, and make a new beginning.

> "And God saw that the wickedness of man *was* great in the
> earth, and *that* every imagination of the thoughts of his heart *was*
> only evil continually. And it *repented* (italics mine) the LORD
> that he had made man on the earth, and it grieved him at his
> heart. . . . The earth also was corrupt before God, and the earth
> was filled with violence " (Gen 6:5-6, 11).

*"The <u>repentance</u> of God is not a change in purpose, but a
change in attitude. Such a change, when it occurs in man,
usually implies a change of mind, hence the word repentance
in human speech represents such a change. God, however,
never changes His mind: His mind is constant, both in love
and holiness. When man changes in his behavior then God
changes His attitude. The expression it repented the LORD is
simply an indication in human language that God's attitude to
man sinning is necessarily different from God's attitude to
man obeying."*[1]

---

[1]Davidson, F., ed. *New Bible Commentary*, Eerdman's Publishing
Company, 1963, p. 83. Not copyrighted, but used by verbal permission
from Eerdmans.

I. NOAH BUILDING THE ARK

Although God found it necessary to destroy the earth with a flood, "Noah found grace in the eyes of the LORD" (Gen. 6:8). God told him to build an ark, to save seed alive to replenish the earth. Without the ark Noah could not have saved one life—not even his own. Noah built the ark, and the ark saved Noah. Both were essential. That is why we list them together as a combination. Each in its own way typified Christ, who of course fulfilled everything they typified, and more.

Noah may have employed many helpers to build that enormous boat, but there is no mention in the text of one other person engaged in the work. Are his helpers kept out of the record because *in building* Noah typifies Christ? Isaiah said of Christ, "I have trodden the winepress alone; of the people there was none with me" (Isa. 63:3)? Salvation was wrought on Calvary by Christ alone, and it saves only those who believe and abide in Christ. The ark which Noah built saved only those who stayed within the ark. Not one soul survived outside the ark.

The first step in building the ark was to cut down the trees for lumber. Cutting those trees to save lives typified the death of Christ, "for he was cut off from the land of the living: for the transgression of my people was he stricken" (Isa. 53:8b).

Noah was instructed to pitch the ark with pitch inside and outside. This is the only place in the Bible where the Hebrew word *kaphar* (# 3722) is translated pitch. Strong defines it as meaning "to cover (spec. with bitumen); fig. to expiate or condone; to placate or cancel." That same word *kaphar* is translated *atonement* seventy times in the Old Testament. So the sealer that waterproofed Noah's ark symbolizes the atonement by which believers are safely sealed in Christ.

All this took many years of labor, but there is no mention of any lapse of time between the instructions and the completion of the ark. We assume that Noah had a hundred and twenty years time to do it (Gen. 6:3), but those years are all summarized in one sentence. "Thus did Noah; according to all that God commanded him, so did he" (6:22). Those few words conceal a hundred years of toil and sweat, plus untold scorn of ungodly neighbors. Then comes the following:

> "And the LORD said unto Noah, Come thou and all thy house into the ark; for thee have I seen righteous before me in this generation. Of every clean beast thou shalt take to thee by sevens, the male and his female: and of the beasts that are not clean by two, the male and his female. Of the fowls also of the air by sevens, the male and the female; to keep seed alive upon the face ofall the earth. For yet seven days, and I will cause it to rain upon the earth forty days and forty nights; and every living substance that I have made will I destroy from off the face of the earth" (Gen 7:1-4).

That is the first occurrence of the word *Come* in the Bible. God was already inside inviting Noah to <u>*Come*</u>, not *Go,* into the ark. More than a year later, when it was time to leave the ark, God told him to <u>*Go*</u> forth of the ark, and of course the LORD came forth with them.

Before the rain began "the LORD shut him in" (7:16). Again we notice the singular personal pronoun *him*. It of course refers to Noah, like elsewhere in these chapters, but it includes his whole family. Noah, as a type of Christ, is here portrayed as the sole actor or participant of all that went on, even as Christ is the sole Activator of our salvation. Believers are His beneficiaries.

Twice we are told that "Noah did according unto all that the LORD commanded him." In that he foreshadowed Jesus, who **always did those things that pleased His Father** (John 8:29).

II. THE ARK TYPIFYING CHRIST

The ark typified Christ in many ways. Some people think it typifies the church. I admit that Noah *building* the ark may symbolize Christ *building* His church. But the church is totally dependent upon Christ for her salvation, even as the lives of Noah and his family depended upon the ark. Salvation is not guaranteed by mere church membership, but by abiding in Christ. Therefore the ark typifies Christ, while *Noah and his family in the ark* typify the *Church in Christ.*

The ark had only one door. That door typified Christ, who says, "I am the door: by me if any man enter in, he shall be saved" (John 10:9). That one door was "set in the side thereof" (Gen. 6:16b), typifying the opened side of Christ, from which the pardoning blood gushed forth (John 19:34) for our salvation.

The ark had only one window. It was at the top, suggesting that we must look up to Christ, "the true Light, which lighteth every man that cometh into the world" (John 1:9).

The ark was waterproof and buoyant. No matter how heavy the torrent nor how turbulent or deep the water, the ark rose triumphantly above it. With no propeller, rudder or sail, the ark of the LORD was safely controlled by the LORD of the ark. Even so Christ rises above whatever the circumstance.

God Never Forgets His Own

"And God remembered Noah, and every living thing, and all the cattle that *was* with him in the ark: and God made a wind to pass over the earth, and the waters assuaged; the fountains also of the deep and the windows of heaven were stopped, and the rain from heaven was restrained; and the waters returned from off the earth continually: and after the end of the hundred and fifty days the waters were abated. And **the ark rested in the seventh month, on the seventeenth day of the month,** upon the mountains of Ararat" (Gen 8:1-4).

The Resurrection Typified

We are especially interested in the ark resting in the seventh month, on the seventeenth day of the month. The seventh month prior to Exodus twelve was the month Abib. When the LORD instituted the passover, He revised the Hebrew calendar, giving the last half of the year preeminence over the first half. We await full revelation of what that signifies, but the transfer is clear.

"This month [Abib, the _seventh_ month] shall be unto you the beginning of months: it shall be the _first_ month of the year to you" (Ex. 12:2). Israel still has two calendars: a civil calendar beginning with Tishri, and a sacred calendar beginning with Abib. Legal documents like property deeds are dated by the civil calendar. Religious feasts and holidays are dated by the sacred calendar.

Our all-wise and all-knowing God had designed that the ark should land on the mountains of Ararat on the seventeenth day of Abib, and that this fact should be recorded in Genesis 8:4. As the waters of the Flood receded, the ark (upheld by the mountain) was lifted out of the water, typifying the resurrection of Christ on the seventeenth day of Abib.

The Passover lamb was to be selected (*identified*) on the tenth day of Abib (Ex. 12:3), kept under close observation for four days, and then killed in the afternoon of the fourteenth day (v. 6). The name Abib (Ex. 13:4; 23:15; 34:18; Dt. 16:1) was changed to Nisan (Neh. 2:1; Esth. 3:7) during the Babylonian Captivity, and Nisan is the name in use today.

Jesus rode into Jerusalem on Palm Sunday, the tenth day of Nisan, on a donkey colt "whereon [heretofore] never man sat." "And the multitudes that went before, and that followed, cried, saying, Hosanna to the son of David: Blessed *is* he that cometh in the name of the Lord; Hosanna in the highest "(Mt. 21:1-9; Mark 11:1-10; Luke 19:29-39; John 12:12-19). This identified Jesus as their Messiah King, selected by the Godhead to be the Ultimate Passover Lamb.

Jesus was not only kept under observation, but was severely tested in those four days. He was challenged by the chief priests and elders (Mt. 21:23– 22:14); the Pharisees with the Herodians (22:15-21); the Sadducees (22:23-33); and the Pharisees with their lawyer (22:34-46) all in one day. Not one defect could they find. He proved Himself to be the perfect Lamb of God!

All of our calendars and most of our man-made books say Jesus was crucified on Friday. It is true that "it was the preparation, that is, the day before the sabbath" (Mark 15:42), "and the sabbath drew on" (Luke 23:54). But that was a special sabbath, more important than the weekly sabbath, "for *that sabbath* was an *high day*" (John 19:31). The day following Passover was *always* "an *holy convocation:* ye shall do no servile work therein" (Lev. 23:5-7; Ex. 12:15-17), no matter what day of the week it was. Therefore *that special sabbath* could well have been on Friday.

Jesus said plainly that "as Jonah was three days and three nights in the whale's belly; so shall the Son of man be three days and three nights in the heart of the earth" (Mt. 12:40). I trust Jesus further than any man-made book or calendar, and I cannot find three days nor nights between Friday evening and Sunday morning. Therefore I am persuaded that Jesus was crucified on Thursday, the fourteenth day of Nisan, rose on the *third day* as He had so often said He would (Mt. 16:21; 17:23; 20:19; 27:63; Mark 9:31; 10:34; Luke 9:22; 18:33; 24:7, 46). That was the first day of the week, the seventeenth day of Abib/Nisan, as typified by Noah's ark landing on that very day.

It was seven months and ten days later before the earth was dry enough for them to leave the ark, where they had been for one year and seventeen days. "And Noah built an altar unto the LORD [the first altar on record]; and took of every clean beast, and of every clean fowl, and offered burnt offerings on the altar" (8:20).

> "And God spake unto Noah, and to his sons with him, saying, And I, behold, I establish my covenant with you, and with your seed after you; and with every living creature that *is* with you, of the fowl, of the cattle, and of every beast of the earth with you; from all that go out of the ark, to every beast of the earth. And I will establish my covenant with you; neither shall all flesh be cut off any more by the waters of a flood; neither shall there any more be a flood to destroy the earth" (Gen 9:8-11).

And as a token of His covenant He put a rainbow in the sky, which testifies today of God's everlasting faithfulness. God cannot lie, and He never breaks a promise!

18

SEEING CHRIST TYPIFIED IN MELCHIZEDEK

Glimpses of His pre-incarnate Glory which He had
with the Father before the world was. John 17:5.

"And Melchizedek king of Salem brought forth bread and
wine: and he *was* the priest of the most high God. And he
blessed him, and said, Blessed *be* Abram of the most high God,
possessor of heaven and earth: and blessed be the most high
God, which hath delivered thine enemies into thy hand. And he
gave him tithes of all" (Gen. 14:18-20).

Melchizedek has the distinction of being the first priest
mentioned in the Bible. He was not only *a* priest, but "*the*
priest of the Most High God" (v. 18). We know of no other
priest in his day. He met Abraham more than 1900 years
before the birth of Christ. By design there is no record of his
race, his ancestry, descendants, or successors, and this is the
only recorded appearance of this remarkable man.

Melchizedek by divine approval is given the unique
honor of foreshadowing the Son of God as both King of
Righteousness and King of Peace, as well as priest. And
Christ's eternal Priesthood is named after him! For "The
LORD hath sworn, and will not repent, Thou art a priest for
ever after the order of Melchizedek" (Ps. 110:4). This is the
second and the last time his name appears in the Old
Testament, but it occurs nine times in the New Testament—

seven times directly associated with the everlasting priest-hood of Christ (Heb. 5:6, 10; 6:20; 7: 11, 15, 17, 21).

Melchizedek is the only man on record who typified Christ by actually serving as both king and priest. The symbolic coronation (Zech. 6:11) of Joshua, the son of Josedech, the official high priest at Jerusalem when the temple was to be rebuilt, was only a symbolic ceremony. It was a prophetic representation of "the man whose name is THE BRANCH." It announced prophetically that Jesus Christ "shall bear the glory, and shall sit and rule upon his throne; and he shall be a priest upon his throne" (vv. 12, 13). Neither of the Joshuas ever reigned as king.

Moses typified Christ as mediator and prophet; Samuel, as prophet, priest, and judge; David, as prophet and king. Under the Mosaic Law there were dire consequences for kings who invaded the priesthood. King Saul lost the kingdom (1 Sam. 13:11-14), and King Uzziah became leprous for the rest of his life (2 Chron. 26:16-21). Many have prefigured Christ either as priest or as king, but only in Melchizedek were both offices actually realized by one man.

> "For this Melchisedec, king of Salem, priest of the most high God, who met Abraham returning from the slaughter of the kings, and blessed him; to whom also Abraham gave a tenth part of all; first being by interpretation King of righteousness, and after that also King of Salem, which is, King of peace; without father, without mother, without descent, having neither beginning of days, nor end of life; but made **like unto** the Son of God; abideth a priest continually" (Heb. 7:1-3).

Melek is a Hebrew word for king, and *tsedeq* is a Hebrew word for righteousness. Therefore, Melchisedec (N. T. spelling) means first "by interpretation King of righteousness, and after that also King of Salem, which is King of peace." Shalom is the Hebrew word for peace. "In Salem also is his tabernacle, and his dwelling place in Zion" (Ps. 76:2). Zion is a part of Salem, now   Jerusalem, the most beseiged and coveted city in the world.

Melchisedec was not literally without father or mother, nor without beginning or end. Eleven times in the Old Testament we read of camels, people, things, or days, said to be "without number," because of their number being untold. Likewise the brass at Solomon's temple "was without weight" (2 Kings 25:16). And David had "prepared . . . brass in abundance without weight"   (1 Chron. 22:3, 14, 16), "for the weight of the brass could not be found out" (2 Chron. 4:18).

Melchisedec "was made **like unto** the Son of God" by leaving his record "without father, without mother, without descent, ... [and as though he had] neither beginning of days, nor end of life." Thus he typifies Jesus who had no beginning—"whose goings forth have been from of old, from everlasting" (Micah 5:2). Melchisedec was both king and priest, but his lineage, his subjects, and his parishioners are all kept out of the record to better typify the Virgin Birth, the *universality* of Christ's *universal* kingdom and His *universal* priesthood.

> "Now consider how great this man *was,* unto whom even the patriarch Abraham gave the tenth of the spoils. And verily they that are of the sons of Levi, who receive the office of the priesthood, have a commandment to take tithes of the people according to the law, that is, of their brethren, though they come out of the loins of Abraham: but he whose descent is not counted from them received tithes of Abraham, and blessed him that had the promises. And without all contradiction the less is blessed of the better" (Heb. 7:4-7).

Although Abraham typifies the Father (Gen. 22:1-17), and "he was called the Friend of God" (James 2:23), this passage puts Melchisedec above the patriarch Abraham. Melchisedec may have been "*the* priest of the most high God" even before Abraham was called out of idolatry. Why did God not choose Melchisedec instead of Abraham?   That would have violated God's promise and marred the type. Both men filled vital positions in God's eternal plan and purpose.   Eight times the Bible speaks of Christ's priesthood being "after the order (or the similitude) of Melchisedec."

Hebrews 7:11-28 goes on to show how much the priesthood of Christ surpasses, as well as supersedes, the Levitical priesthood.

"If therefore perfection were by the Levitical priesthood, (for under it the people received the law,) what further need *was there* that another priest should rise after the order of Melchisedec, and not be called after the order of Aaron? For the priesthood being changed, there is made of necessity a change also of the law.

"For he of whom these things are spoken pertaineth to another tribe, of which no man gave attendance at the altar. For *it is* evident that our Lord sprang out of Juda; of which tribe Moses spake nothing concerning priesthood.

"And it is yet far more evident: for that after the similitude of Melchisedec there ariseth another priest, who is made, not after the law of a carnal commandment, but after the power of an endless life. For he testifieth, Thou *art* a priest for ever after the order of Melchisedec.

"For there is verily a disannulling of the commandment going before for the weakness and unprofitableness thereof. For the law made nothing perfect, but the bringing in of a better hope *did;* by the which we draw nigh unto God.

"And inasmuch as not without an oath *he was made priest:* (For those priests were made without an oath; but this with an oath by him that said unto him, The Lord sware and will not repent, Thou *art* **a priest for ever after the order of Melchisedec:**) by so much was Jesus made a surety of a better testament.

"And they truly were many priests, because they were not suffered to continue by reason of death: but this *man,* because he **continueth ever,** hath **an unchangeable priesthood.** Wherefore he is able also to save them to the uttermost that come unto God by him, seeing he ever liveth to make intercession for them.

"For such an high priest became us, *who is* holy, harmless, undefiled, separate from sinners, and made higher than the heav-

ens; who needeth not daily, as those high priests, to offer up sacrifice, first for his own sins, and then for the people's: for this he
did once, when he offered up himself. For the law maketh men
high priests which have infirmity; but the word of the oath,
which was since the law, *maketh* the Son, who is **consecrated
for evermore**" (Heb. 7:11-28).

Melchisedec was greater than Abraham (7:4, 7), but it is
evident that Melchisedec was only a shadow of the
Substance. It is **Christ** who ever liveth to make intercession
for the saints.

19

SEEING CHRIST TYPIFIED IN
ABRAHAM AND ISAAC

Glimpses of His Pre-incarnate Glory which He had
with the Father before the world was. John 17:5.

I. ABRAHAM

Abram was born and raised in idolatry, in a city where
"they served other gods" (Josh. 24:2, 14). Collective evi-
dences[1] suggest that he was nearly seventy years old when
"the God of glory appeared unto him" (Acts 7:2-4), calling
him to a fourfold separation.

> " Get thee **out of thy country**, and **from thy kindred**, and
> **from thy father's house**, [and] **unto a land** that I will show
> thee: and I will make of thee a great nation, and I will bless thee,
> and make thy name great; and thou shalt be a blessing" (Gen.
> 12:1-2).

Biblical separation is always twofold: something to be
separated *from*, and **Someone** to be separated *unto*. God
wanted Abram separated from an idolatrous environment, but
that alone is never enough. He wanted him to be fully **set
apart for God**. It took about thirty years to accomplish that.
But finally he was so rapt up with submission and obedience
to God that God Himself called him "Abraham my friend"
(Isa. 41:8; 2 Chron. 20:7; James 2:23). No other mortal is

---

[1]Terah died in Haran at the age of 205 years (Gen. 11:32), after which
Abram was 75 (Gen. 12:4).

given that title. His final relationship with God uniquely typified Christ Incarnate.

Abram's wife, Sarai, was barren, and at their age it looked hopeless for them to ever have children. Yet God promised to make of Abram a great nation, which would require many descendants. But Abram would first need to settle in the country which God would show him. We don't know whether they started the next morning or the next year. We only know that Abram, Sarai, his father Terah, and his nephew Lot, departed from Ur, "and they came unto Haran, and _dwelt there_" (Gen. 11:31b).

That was only partial obedience (about 25%). Abram had gotten out of his country, but was not yet separated from his father's house, nor from his kindred, nor was Haran the country he was to go to. It is uncertain, but generally believed, they may have lived in Haran about five years. Abram did not leave Haran to go on into Canaan until his father Terah had died (Acts 7:4).

> "And Abram was seventy and five years old when he departed out of Haran. And Abram took Sarai his wife, and Lot his brother's son, and all their substance that they had gathered, and the souls that they had gotten in Haran; and they went forth to go into the land of Canaan; and into the land of Canaan they came" (Gen. 12:4b, 5).

What they had _gathered_ and _gotten_ in Haran undoubtedly took several years. When Abram had lived in Canaan for several years, and still had no son, we can almost hear the pleading tone of his voice when he said,

> "Lord GOD [_Adonai Jehovah_], what wilt thou give me, seeing I go childless, . . . to me thou hast given no seed: and, lo, one born in my house is mine heir" (Gen. 15:2, 3).

Then the LORD renewed His promise (15:5-7), adding several details, and confirmed it with a ceremonial oath (15:8-17).

After ten years in the land of Canaan (16:3), Abram being 85 years old and Sarai possibly 76, their patience was wearing thin. So they tried to help God make His promise good. They definitely understood that Abram was to have a son, but did not yet understand that he also had to be the son of Sarai.

> "And Sarai said unto Abram, Behold now, the LORD hath restrained me from bearing: I pray thee, go in unto my maid; it may be that I may obtain children by her. And Abram hearkened to the voice of Sarai. . . . And he went in unto Hagar, and she conceived: and when she saw that she had conceived, her mistress was despised in her eyes. And Sarai said unto Abram, My wrong *be* upon thee: I have given my maid into thy bosom; and when she saw that she had conceived, I was despised in her eyes: the LORD judge between me and thee" (Gen. 16:2, 4-5).

A son was born, but he was not the son that God had promised. Their humanistic effort sparked a conflict that surfaced first on the marital level (Gen. 16:5), grew into a family conflict that brought suffering to their whole family (21:9-21), and finally mushroomed into an international conflict that will probably rage in the Middle East until Jesus Christ returns.

Abram was eighty-six years old when Ishmael was born (Gen. 16:16). There is no evidence of any further word from the LORD until Abram was ninety-nine (17:1). Apparently God withheld all communication those thirteen years, until Abram and Sarai learned to lay hold on God's promise by faith, with no evidence in sight. Then, for the first time, God introduced Himself to Abram as the Almighty God (*El-Shaddai* – discussed earlier in *chapter five).*

> "And Abram fell on his face: and God talked with him, saying, As for me, behold, my covenant *is* with thee, and thou shalt be a father of many nations. Neither shall thy name any more be called Abram, but thy name shall be Abraham; for a father of many nations have I made thee. And I will make thee exceeding fruitful, and I will make nations of thee, and kings shall come out of thee. And I will establish my covenant between me and thee and thy seed after thee in their generations for an everlasting

covenant, to be a God unto thee, and to thy seed after thee. And I will give unto thee, and to thy seed after thee, the land wherein thou art a stranger, all the land of Canaan, for an everlasting possession; and I will be their God" (Gen. 17:3-8).

God changed their names from Abram to Abraham, and Sarai to Sarah, and instituted circumcision as a token of His covenant with the nation He was about to establish (17:9-14). Ishmael was thirteen years old, and Abraham had become so attached to him that he pleaded, "O that Ishmael might live before thee" (17:18). Abraham, Ishmael, and every male of Abraham's house were cicumcised in the selfsame day (17:23-27). It was their token of God's covenant with them.

II. ISAAC

The typology of Isaac sprouted roots in Abram's call to separation, thirty years before Isaac was born. His early types of Christ involved Abram as much as Isaac. The promise of his birth, the waiting, and the required preparation all fell upon Abram. Isaac's primary role the first forty years of his life was that of submission, and Abram certainly shared in that as well. I combine them in one chapter because as a father and son team they typified God the Father and Christ the Son, especially in offering up Isaac and in obtaining a bride for Isaac.

Named Before Birth

"And God said, **Sarah thy wife** shall bear thee a son indeed; and thou shalt **call his name Isaac**: and I will establish my covenant with him for an everlasting covenant, *and* with his seed after him. And as for Ishmael, I have heard thee: Behold, I have blessed him, and will make him fruitful, and will multiply him exceedingly; twelve princes shall he beget, and I will make him a great nation. **But my covenant will I establish with Isaac, which Sarah shall bear unto thee at this set time in the next year**" (Gen. 17:19-21).

The details were spelled out explicitly. Then they knew that the promised son will be born of Sarah. God Himself named him Isaac, a year before his birth. That foreshadows God's own long-promised Son, named more than seven hundred years in advance (Isa. 7:14).

His Miraculous Birth

Apparently God had been waiting for two things: (1) for Abraham to become impotent, so that Isaac would be a double miracle, (2) and for their faith to become strong enough to rest in God alone, when there remained **no more hope in the flesh**! (This, and its confirmation in the New Testament, are also discussed in chapter five on El-Shaddai.)

God had designed that Isaac should have a miraculous birth (one that was humanly impossible), to typify the Virgin Birth of Jesus Christ. And as for Ishmael, in spite of him being brought in apart from God's initial plan, God blessed him greatly and made ample room for him and his descendants. That did not undo the consequential reaping for man-made errors of the flesh, but God used it in the New Testament to allegorize the importance of being born again— "not of blood, nor of the will of the flesh, nor of the will of man, **but of God**" (John 1:13).

"For it is written, that Abraham had two sons, the one by a bondmaid, the other by a freewoman. But he *who was* of the bondwoman was born **after the flesh**; but he of the freewoman *was* **by promise**. Which things are an allegory: for these are the two covenants; the one from the mount Sinai, which gendereth to bondage, which is Agar. For this Agar is mount Sinai in Arabia, and answereth to Jerusalem which now is, and is in bondage with her children.

"But Jerusalem which is above is free, which is the mother of us all. For it is written, Rejoice, *thou* barren that bearest not; break forth and cry, thou that travailest not: for the desolate hath many more children than she which hath an husband.

"Now we, brethren, as Isaac was, are the children of promise. But as then he that was **born after the flesh** persecuted him *that was born* **after the Spirit**, even so *it is* now. Nevertheless what saith the scripture? Cast out the bondwoman

102 SEEING CHRIST IN THE OLD TESTAMENT

and her son: for the son of the bondwoman shall not be heir with the son of the freewoman. So then, brethren, we are not children of the bondwoman, but of the free" (Gal. 4:22-31).

"For what the law could not do, in that it was weak through the flesh, God sending his own Son in the likeness of sinful flesh, and for sin, condemned sin in the flesh: that the righteousness of the law might be fulfilled in us, who walk not after the flesh, but after the Spirit. For they that are after the flesh do mind the things of the flesh; but they that are after the Spirit the things of the Spirit" (Rom. 8:3-5).

Offered Up by His Father

Nowhere did Isaac typify Christ more beautifully than when he was "offered up" (Heb. 11:17) by his father "in the mount of the LORD" (Gen. 22:14), and what followed thereafter. God was voluntarily committed to offer the greatest of all sacrifices on Mount Calvary. But He wanted Abraham (a type of God the Father) and Isaac (a type of Christ) to experience a *preview* of that great event. So He called Abraham and said,

"Take now thy son, thine only son Isaac, whom thou lovest, and get thee into the land of Moriah; and offer him there for a burnt offering upon **one of the mountains** *[unnamed]* which I will tell thee of" (Gen. 22:2).

By that time Abraham had learned to do whatever God asked of him, "accounting that God was able to raise [Isaac] up, even from the dead" (Heb. 11:19). So he rose up early, **split the wood** (prefiguring the death that was supposed to follow), *presumably* loaded it on the donkey, took Isaac and two young men, and departed for that unnamed mountain God would show him.. On **the third day** he saw the place afar off (far enough that the young men would not witness the scene).

"And Abraham said unto his young men, Abide ye here with the ass; and **I and the lad** will go yonder and worship, and **come again to you**" (v. 5).

Notice his confidence that "the lad" would come home with him. The age of "the lad" is not given, but I am convinced he was fully grown, perhaps comparable to the age that Jesus was when He became the ultimate "offering for sin."[2]

Observe that Abraham *laid the wood on Isaac.* Wood often typifies the humanity of Jesus (like in the Ark of the Covenant). Here it may typify both His humanity and Him bearing His cross. So it was appropriate for Isaac to carry the wood. Abraham, who represents the Father, *took the fire in his hand, and a knife.* Fire symbolizes Spirit (Mt. 3:11; John 4:24), divine judgment (Gen. 3:24; 19:24), and acceptance of the sacrifice (Lev. 9:24; Judges 6:21; 1 Kings 18:38; 1 Chron. 21:26;   2 Chron. 7:1). The *knife,* like the *flaming sword* (Gen. 3:24), also implied judgment, perhaps on a more intimate (Father-Son) level. For Abraham to carry the wood, and Isaac to carry the fire and knife, would have marred the type.

"So they went both of them together" (Gen. 22:6 and 8). What transpired on that mount was a sacred transaction between *father and son alone,* yet with <u>*both of them together*</u>! It prefigured that **greater transaction** which **Father** and **Son** wrought <u>together</u> on Calvary, when "God was in Christ reconciling the world unto himself "(2 Cor. 5:19).

> "And they came to the place which God had told him of; and Abraham built an altar there, and laid the wood in order, and bound Isaac his son, and laid him on the altar upon the wood" (Gen. 22:9).

That verse leaves more untold than is verbalized!   It depicts that moment in eternity past when our pre-incarnate Saviour freely committed Himself to be the sacrificial Lamb

---

[2]When Benjamin was in his thirties his brother Judah referred to him as "a little one" (Gen. 44:20). Less than a year later that "little one" took his ten sons along to Egypt (46:21). In Genesis 24 Isaac took Rebekah as his wife, at which time he was forty years old (25:20). So he could easily have been in his early thirties when he was "offered up" (22:12). That would compare with Jesus' age when He was offered up.

of God. We can rest assured that when Abraham had the altar prepared, he and Isaac had a tender and touching discussion and a mutual agreement about their commitment to the will of God.

Isaac was in the prime of his life. If he would have shown resistance, his aged father could not have bound him. A physical tussle would have ruined the picture! As a type of Christ, Isaac must have demonstrated a willingness similar to that of Christ. Binding Isaac was typical of binding Jesus (Mark 15:1; John 18:12). Both were controlled by *heart ties* far superior to *hand cuffs*. External bonds were unnecessary—utterly powerless in Jesus' case (Mt. 26:53).

The Bible says Abraham "offered up Isaac" (Heb. 11:17). In his heart and in the eyes of God he had done so. Therefore, right up to the time when the upraised knife was stayed by "the angel of the LORD" calling out of heaven (Gen. 22:11), Isaac typified Christ being offered by His Father. At that moment (by his release and the ram being offered in his stead) he also became a type of believers released and redeemed by the vicarious sacrifice of Christ.

Typifying the Ascension and Second Coming of Christ

Isaac continued to typify Christ in another aspect. Notice that his return to Beersheba is kept completely out of the record (obviously by design). Of course he returned as Abraham had suggested he would (Gen. 22:5). Surely Isaac, Sarah's only son, was a prominent figure at her funeral (Gen. 23). Surely Abraham had Isaac's consent to send his eldest servant, to find a wife for Isaac (24:2).

But from the time when Abraham had *not withheld his son* (22:16), Isaac is kept (*as it were*) unseen during all this time. We read nothing of Isaac until he came "*at the eventide* . . . and, behold, the camels were coming" (24:62-63). Abraham's most trusted servant, "that ruled over all that he had," had brought Rebekah to be Isaac's wife.

Christ was also offered "on the mount of the LORD" (22:14), where "the LORD beheld, . . . and said to the angel that destroyed, *It is enough, stay now thy hand*" (1 Chron. 21:14-16). That is also where Solomon built his temple, "in mount Moriah, where the LORD appeared unto David . . . in the threshing floor of Ornan the Jebusite" (2 Chron. 3:1).

Christ rose from the dead on the third day (verified ten times in the Scriptures), and in the next forty days He was seen by believers on ten or eleven different occasions. After which He was taken up to heaven, never again to make a public appearance until *the evening of time.* The Holy Spirit (typified by Abraham's *unnamed* servant) has been sent to obtain a Bride for Christ (Mt. 9:15;   25:1, 6, 10; John 3:29; Rom. 7:4; 2 Cor. 11:2; Eph. 5:25-27; Rev. 19:7). The Holy Spirit will bring Christ's Bride (the Church) *at the eventide of time,* and Christ will reappear to receive His Bride to Himself, "and so shall we ever be with the Lord" (1 Thess. 4:16-17)!

> "Repent ye therefore, and be converted, that your sins may be blotted out, when the times of refreshing shall come from the presence of the Lord; and he shall send Jesus Christ, which before was preached unto you: whom the heaven must receive until the times of restitution of all things, which God hath spoken by the mouth of all his holy prophets since the world began" (Acts 3:19-21).

Isaac typified Christ in Other Ways

* Both Isaac and Christ were appointed heir of all their father's possessions (Gen. 24:36; 25:5. Cf. Heb. 1:2).

* Isaac alone of the Patriarchs is never seen beyond the borders of the promised land. This may typify Jesus never venturing outside the border of His Father's will.

* Eight times Isaac appears in connection with wells of water. Genesis 24:62; 25:11; 26:18, 19, 20, 21, 22, 25. One flowed with "springing water "(26:19), evidently an artesian well. Other translations say, running, or

flowing, and Luther's German says "Living Water." As the man of wells, Isaac typifies Christ, who is indeed the source of Living Water (John 4:10, 11; 7:38).

Human Error Never Typifies Christ

Abraham typified God the Father and Isaac typified Christ the Son, only in certain aspects. In other aspects they had the natural signs of fallen man. Both lied to Abimelech, presenting their wife as their sister. "Isaac loved Esau because he did eat of his venison: but Rebekah loved Jacob" (Gen. 25:28). Partiality is incompatible with Christ, and its wedges brought many heartaches upon this family.

May we learn from their mistakes and be instructed by their virtues.

20

SEEING CHRIST TRANSFORMING JACOB

Glimpses of His pre-incarnate glory which He had
with the Father before the world was. John 17:5

Abraham, "the Friend of God" (James 2:23: Isa. 41:8),
typified the Father offering His Son. Isaac, in his miraculous
birth and the first forty years of his life, typified the birth, crucifixion, ascension, and second coming of Christ. But Jacob
was different. He demonstrates the natural man's need for
Christ, the law of sowing and reaping, and Christ's faithful
persistence in transforming *death traps* into *life*. God knows
how much we need that lesson!

Jacob was the **second-born** son of Isaac. There are a
number of occasions where the second son was given preeminence over the first. For example: Abel, Isaac, Jacob,
Ephraim (Gen. 4:4; 17:21; 25:23; 48:18, 19) and others.
They impress upon us our need for a **second birth**. Our first
birth was a physical entry which brought us into this world.
But for adults to be children of God, we "**must be born
again**," . . . "not of blood, nor of the will of the flesh, nor of
the will of man, but of God" (John 3:5-7; 1:13). Consider
also 1 Corinthians 15:45-50.

The Natural Man

"Jacob was a *plain* man, dwelling in tents." Other translations use adjectives like *mild* (NKJ), *quiet* (NIV), *peaceful*
(NASB). He was conscientious, prayerful, and gentle, but

107

also self-willed and self-centered—frequently looking for personal gain. He was a living demonstration of our two natures, both bad and good—our *old* and *new* natures.

When his brother Esau was hungry and faint, Jacob bargained with him for the birthright, and got it. Later he violated his own conscience by helping his mother to deceive his father, and even lied to obtain his father's major blessing (Gen. 27:5-24).

> "And Esau hated Jacob because of the blessing wherewith his father blessed him: and Esau said in his heart, The days of mourning for my father are at hand; *then will I slay my brother Jacob*" (Gen. 27:41) . (Emphasis added.)

Sowing and Reaping

Jacob's self-centered aggressiveness could not bypass the law of sowing and reaping . The bitter hatred of Esau cost Jacob twenty years in exile from the Promised Land, in a land that cherished idols. There he was deceived by Laban, who gave him Leah instead of Rachel, based on what Laban called the rights of the first-born. With a tinge of bitterness, Jacob spoke later of Laban having "changed my wages ten times." He also suffered from family conflicts between Rachel and Leah, and later between his sons. His most bitter harvest came when his sons, with the blood-stained coat of Joseph, deceived him even more craftily than he had deceived his father.

While serving Laban, Jacob tried various schemes in an effort to increase his own flock. God certainly blessed him, not because of, but in spite of his scheming. But he lost the favor of Laban's sons. When Jacob received word from the Lord to go back to Canaan he took his family and flocks and "stole away unawares to Laban" (Gen. 31:20). When Laban learned that Jacob had fled, he and his brethren pursued him seven days journey, and overtook him.

Unknown to Jacob, Rachel had stolen Laban's gods, and Laban intended to recover them. But God had warned Laban in a dream not to speak evil to Jacob. Laban searched every tent, but found them not. Rachel, by deception and lying, out-witted them both.

> "Jacob was wroth, and chided with Laban: and Jacob answered and said to Laban, What *is* my trespass? what *is* my sin, that thou hast so hotly pursued after me? Whereas thou hast searched all my stuff, what hast thou found of all thy household stuff? set *it* here before my   brethren and thy brethren, that they may judge betwixt us both" (Gen. 31:36-37).

Rachel had hidden those images "in the camel's furniture, and sat upon them" so that Laban did not find them. Now Jacob had said to Laban, "With whomsoever thou findest thy gods, **let him not live**." Then we wonder why Rachel died so young (Gen. 35:16-19).

When Laban and Jacob had made a covenant of peace, Laban departed, and Jacob's thoughts turned toward the twen-ty-year estrangement between him and his twin brother. He sent messengers to Esau, saying,

> "I have sent to tell my lord, that I may find grace in thy sight. The messengers returned to Jacob, saying, We came to thy brother Esau, and also he cometh to meet thee, and four hundred men with him. Then Jacob was greatly afraid and distressed" (Gen. 32:5b-7a).

Jacob sent another delegation, with a present of 580 head of livestock for Esau, to obtain grace in his sight (Gen. 32:13-20). He divided his people, his flocks, herds, and camels into two groups, and prayed earnestly that if Esau smote one group the other would escape. Obviously Esau was not bring-ing four hundred men as a welcoming committee! That night was Jacob's *Gethsemane.*

Transforming Jacob

The *man* who wrestled all night with Jacob (Gen. 32:24-32) was undoubtedly Christ Himself. Compare Hosea 12:3-6. He could have disabled Jacob totally with one word of His mouth, but His purpose was spiritual. He doesn't want puppets, but people who obey willingly. Therefore He dealt gently with Jacob's physical body, but wrestled vigorously with his stubborn self-will. The spiritual contest towered far above the physical.

At daybreak, seeing that Jacob's will remained unconquered, He simply touched the hollow of Jacob's thigh, and his hip was out of joint. No longer could he walk like a soldier ready for battle, but with a limp that mellowed the heart of Esau. His limp was the *blessing* he needed that day.

Recognizing the divine nature of his "antagonist," Jacob clung to Him in desperation, saying, "I will not let thee go, except thou bless me." The Lord blessed him, saying, "Thy name shall be called no more Jacob [supplanter], but Israel [prince]: for as a prince hast thou power with God and with men, and hast prevailed. . . . And he blessed him there. And Jacob called the name of the place Peniel: for I have seen God face to face, and my life is preserved" (Gen. 32:28-30).

In all of these experiences Christ was working to transform the character of Jacob. In John 1:51 Jesus identified Himself as the One represented by the ladder in Jacob's dream at Luz (Gen. 28:12-19). Jacob didn't know it, but Christ had actually watched over Jacob every day of his life.

Although, prior to Pentecost, saints of God did not really experience the new birth, Jacob's experience at Peniel was a beautiful *foreshadow* of the new birth. From that time forth he was a different man. The work of Christ was more evident in his life, as the touching scene of his personal reconciliation with Esau reveals. Prevailing by servitude, he was now rightly called Israel.

> "Jacob lifted up his eyes, and looked, and, behold, Esau came, and with him four hundred men. And he divided the children unto Leah, and unto Rachel, and unto the two handmaids. And he put the handmaids and their children foremost, and Leah and her children after, and Rachel and Joseph hindermost. And he [*limping*] passed over before them, and bowed himself to the ground seven times, until he came near to his brother.

"And Esau ran to meet him, and embraced him, and fell on his neck, and kissed him: and they wept. And he lifted up his eyes, and saw the women and the children; and said, Who *are* those with thee? And he said, The children which God hath graciously given thy servant.

"Then the handmaidens came near, they and their children, and they bowed themselves. And Leah also with her children came near, and bowed themselves: and after came Joseph near and Rachel, and they bowed themselves.

"And [Esau] said, What *meanest* thou by all this drove which I met? And [Jacob] said, *These are* to find grace in the sight of my lord. And Esau said, I have enough, my brother; keep that thou hast unto thyself.

"And Jacob said, Nay, I pray thee, if now I have found grace in thy sight, then receive my present at my hand: for therefore I have seen thy face, as though I had seen the face of God, and thou wast pleased with me. Take, I pray thee, my blessing that is brought to thee; because God hath dealt graciously with me, and because I have enough. And he urged him, and he took *it.*

"And [Esau] said, Let us take our journey, and let us go, and I will go before thee. And [Jacob] said unto him, My lord knoweth that the children *are* tender, and the flocks and herds with young *are* with me: and if men should overdrive them one day, all the flock will die. Let my lord, I pray thee, pass over before his servant: and I will lead on softly, according as the cattle that goeth before me and the children be able to endure, until I come unto my lord unto Seir.

"And Esau said, Let me now leave with thee *some* of the folk that *are* with me. And [Jacob] said, What needeth it? let me find grace in the sight of my lord. So Esau returned that day on his way unto Seir. And Jacob journeyed to Succoth, and built him a house" (Gen. 33:1-17a).

Jacob bowing himself to the ground seven times, and limping every time he rose, melted the bitterness in Esau's heart. The *death trap* was closed. Jacob's life was preserved and enhanced. What a sad ending this story might have had if our pre-incarnate Christ had not wrestled with Jacob's will the previous night!

Still Reaping

But their *personal* reconciliation could not undo all the wide-spread damage. Those twenty years of bitterness (Heb. 12:14-17) had taken root in Esau's extensive family. After all, Esau had taken two wives when he was forty (Gen. 26:34), the third one when he was in his seventies (28:9), and by this time he must have been ninety-seven.[1] With possibly scores of grandchildren, his animosity had already spread to tribal dimensions. That tribal enmity, with 3500 years of growth, has developed into international conflicts that will not find permanent peace until Jesus comes!

The Founding and Future of Israel

When the name Jacob (*supplanter*) was changed to Israel (*prince of God*), the Lord said, "Thy name shall be called no more Jacob, but Israel." That is the first occurrence of the name Israel, after which the name *Jacob* still appears 237 times in the Old Testament. Frequently it applies to his descendants, national Israel (unregenerate, and often disobedient). *Israel* appears 2491 times in the Old Testament, and seventy-five times in the New Testament. In the New Testament, *Jacob* means either the man Jacob or his offspring, and *Israel* means either the people or the Land.

At this writing God is still wrestling with national Israel—called *Jacob* in this passage:

---

[1] The age of Esau, Jacob's twin, can be calculated by information we have about Joseph. Joseph was born at the end of Jacob's fourteen years of service with Laban, his dowry for Leah and Rachel (Gen. 30:25-26). He was thirty when he interpreted Pharaoh's dreams (41:46). Then after seven years of plenty (41:29), plus two years of famine (45:11), Joseph was thirty-nine. At that time Jacob was a hundred and thirty (47:9), minus thirty-nine makes Jacob ninety-one when Joseph was born. Then he served six more years for the flock (31:41) before returning to Canaan. Thus Jacob and Esau were about ninety-seven years of age when they were reconciled.

For "there shall come out of Sion the Deliverer, and shall turn away ungodliness from **Jacob**: For this *is* my covenant unto them, when I shall take away their sins. As concerning the gospel, *they are* enemies for your sakes: but as touching the election, *they are* beloved for the fathers' sakes. For the gifts and calling of God *are* without repentance.

"For as ye in times past have not believed God, yet have now obtained mercy through their unbelief: even so have these also now not believed, that through your mercy they also may obtain mercy. For God hath concluded them all in unbelief, that he might have mercy upon all.

"O the depth of the riches both of the wisdom and knowledge of God! how unsearchable *are* his judgments, and his ways past finding out" (Rom. 11:26b-33).

Not until they find their *hip out of joint,* and see Him whom they have pierced , will they collectively acknowledge Him as Lord and Master. Then, says the Lord,

"I will pour upon the house of David, and upon the inhabitants of Jerusalem, the spirit of grace and of supplications: and they shall look upon me whom they have pierced, and they shall mourn for him, as one mourneth for *his* only *son,* and shall be in bitterness for him, as one that is in bitterness for *his* firstborn" (Zech. 12:10).

A careful and prayerful study of Zechariah 12, 13, and 14 gives glimpses of Christ still wrestling with Israel. "That day," repeated seventeen times in those forty-four verses, is of major importance. God is often grieved but never defeated. His eternal purposes may even be delayed and reprogramed (Nu. 14:26-45), but never cancelled. His promises never fail.

21

SEEING CHRIST TYPIFIED IN JOSEPH

Glimpses of His sufferings in the flesh
leading to even greater Eternal Glory

Part One: Both Suffered in the Flesh

Joseph is the last of Israel's patriarchs recorded in Genesis, and to him is given more space than to any of his predecessors. Joseph's background was adorned with much prenatal prayer. His great-grandmother Sara had been barren until she was ninety. His grandmother Rebekah was barren the first twenty years of married life; and his mother Rachel, for six years. While Rachel's suffering for lack of children was much the shortest, she expressed it more intensely. "Give me children, or else I die" (Gen. 30:1), shows the intensity of her cry!

God remembered Rachel, heard her prayer, and gave her a son. She named him Joseph, and said, "The Lord shall add to me another son" (30:24). God gave her Benjamin after waiting another six or seven years, but she died in giving birth to him (35:18).

Thus Joseph, who never saw his grandmother Rebekkah, was left motherless in his early childhood. Is that why Jacob lavished so much love on Joseph? Another less legitimate reason was that Joseph was the firstborn son of Jacob's favorite wife. Favoritism and competition, very evident in this family from its very beginning, are problems that naturally

accompany polygamy. Out of this turmoil God raised up
Joseph to typify His own beloved Son in more ways than any
other Bible character. Joseph's name leads the list of the generations of Jacob.

> "These *are* the generations of Jacob. **Joseph,** *being* seven-
> teen years old, was feeding the flock with his brethren; and the
> lad *was* with the sons of Bilhah, and with the sons of Zilpah, his
> father's wives: and Joseph brought unto his father their evil
> report. Now Israel loved Joseph more than all his children,
> because he *was* the son of his old age: and he made him a coat
> of *many* colours. And when his brethren saw that their father
> loved him more than all his brethren, they hated him, and could
> not speak peaceably unto him" (Gen. 37:2-4).

What Jacob meant for Joseph's benefit became the source
of his severest tests, preparing him for future fame. Joseph's
prophetic dreams, which in his youthful innocence and sin-
cerity he shared with his brothers, greatly agitated the already
tense situation (37:5-11). Joseph could have avoided some of
this agitation by keeping his dreams to himself, but possibly
God meant for his brethren to know about them too. At least
his father pondered the matter. And, in Egypt, when the
dreams were finally fulfilled, his brothers remembered them
effectively.

Undoubtedly Joseph often pondered those dreams during
his thirteen years of bondage, first as a slave and then as a
prisoner. We may wonder whether they served as a source of
inspiration and comfort to him, or a source of frustration. I
like to think the Lord used them as a ray of hope and encouragement. We know not how many secret messages God may
have conveyed to Joseph in his most trying hours.

Joseph's last assignment given by his father Jacob was an
errand of concern for his brothers. Apparently the ten oldest
sons had taken their father's flock to feed at Shechem. That
is where Simeon and Levi had earlier smitten all the males in
the village (Gen. 34:25-30), and the sons of Jacob had taken
all their possessions. Even their little ones and their wives
they had taken captive, and spoiled the whole village, because

Shechem had defiled their sister Dinah. At that time Jacob was troubled, fearing retaliation from the inhabitants of the land. He had reasons to be concerned about how his sons fared at Shechem.

Joseph may have been apprehensive too, not so much because of the inhabitants of the land, but because he knew how his brothers hated him. Nevertheless his immediate response was, "Here am I" (37:13). Being submissive and dutiful, he went most willingly.

Joseph was, of course, surpassed by his great Antitype. Jesus also willingly submitted to being sent by His Father, and came seeking His brethren. "He came unto his own, and his own received him not. But as many as received him, to them gave he power to become the sons of God" (John 1:11, 12). Joseph's brothers saw the day when God used Joseph to save their lives.

When Joseph got to Shechem his brothers were not there. To a man he met in the field, Joseph said, "I seek my brethren" (37:16). Informed that they had gone to Dothan, he went and found them there. What a disappointment awaited him when he met them! They conspired against him, stripped him of his treasured coat, and most of them wanted to slay him.

> "And Reuben said unto them, Shed no blood, *but* cast him into this pit that *is* in the wilderness, and lay no hand upon him; that he might rid him out of their hands, to deliver him to his father again" (Gen. 37:22).

Consenting to Reuben, their oldest brother, they cast Joseph alive into the pit, "and they sat down to eat bread."

But Judah, foreshadowing Judas Iscariot, said, "What profit *is it* if we slay our brother, and conceal his blood? Come, and let us sell him to the Ishmeelites, and let not our hand be upon him; for he *is* our brother *and* our flesh" (37:26-27). The brothers agreed. So they lifted Joseph out of the pit, and sold him to the Ishmeelites for twenty *pieces* of silver. And the Ishmeelites took him down to Egypt.

"And Reuben returned unto the pit; and, behold, Joseph *was* not in the pit; and he rent his clothes. And he returned unto his brethren, and said, The child *is* not; and I, whither shall I go?

"And they took Joseph's coat, and killed a kid of the goats, and dipped the coat in the blood; And they sent the coat of *many* colours, and they brought *it* to their father; and said, This have we found: know now whether it *be* thy son's coat or no. And he knew it, and said, *It is* my son's coat; an evil beast hath devoured him; Joseph is without doubt rent in pieces. And Jacob rent his clothes, and put sackcloth upon his loins, and mourned for his son many days" (Gen. 37:29-34).

The law of sowing and reaping did double duty. Jacob deceived his father to obtain the major blessing , then spent twenty years reaping with Laban, and practicing more deception. He was reaping when Laban gave him Leah to wife, instead of Rachel for whom he had bargained.

He was sowing when he sought to gain more cattle by laying striped poplar and chesnut rods in the watering trough when the flock came to drink (Gen. 30:37-43). He reaped bountifully when his sons deceived him with the blood stained coat of Joseph. And his sons for twenty years suffered a guilty conscience for having sold their brother and deceived their father. They confessed it among themselves during their dilemma in Egypt and it all came to light when Joseph revealed himself to them.

"Joseph was brought down to Egypt; and Potiphar, an officer of Pharaoh, captain of the guard, an Egyptian, bought him of the hands of the Ishmeelites, which had brought him down thither. And the LORD was with Joseph, and he was a prosperous man; and he was in the house of his master the Egyptian. And his master saw that the LORD *was* with him, and that the LORD made all that he did to prosper in his hand. And Joseph found grace in his sight, and he served him: and he made him overseer over his house, and all *that* he had he put into his hand.

"And it came to pass from the time *that* he had made him overseer in his house, and over all that he had, that the LORD blessed the Egyptian's house for Joseph's sake; and the blessing of the LORD was upon all that he had in the house, and in the field. And he left all that he had in Joseph's hand; and he knew not ought he had, save the bread which he did eat. And Joseph was *a* goodly *person,* and well favoured" (Gen. 39:1-6).

Joseph, serving as a bond servant to the Captain of Pharaoh's guard, proved himself faithful and trustworthy in every way. Even the Egyptian's household was blessed for Joseph's sake. He typified Jesus whose very presence is an innate blessing to everyone with whom He abides. Whatever Joseph did the Lord caused it to prosper in his hand. He was honest, true and unblamable in his moral life, and very efficient in his assignments.

Even his master's wife (in spite of whatever authority she had, and although she tried it day by day) could not seduce him to sin. He steadfastly refused to "do this great wickedness, and sin against God." When "she caught him by his garment" in an effort to force him, he left the garment in her hand and fled out of the house. In frustrated anger she lied to her husband, and by false accusation caused Joseph to be cast into prison. Genesis 39:7-20.

"But the LORD was with Joseph, and showed him mercy, and gave him favour in the sight of the keeper of the prison. And the keeper of the prison committed to Joseph's hand all the prisoners that *were* in the prison; and whatsoever they did there, he was the doer *of it.* The keeper of the prison looked not to any thing *that was* under his hand; because the LORD was with him, and *that* which he did, the LORD made *it* to prosper" (Gen. 39:21-23).

Friction that would frazzle the toughest fabric only polishes a diamond. God was certainly polishing Joseph to be a jewel of the highest quality. Every test brought out a new luster in his character, and prepared him for higher service. As a prisoner he impressed the keeper of the prison with his impeccable integrity, so that he committed "to Joseph's hand all the prisoners that were in the prison." That was quite an order for a slave boy in his mid-twenties.

Sometime thereafter the chief of the king's butlers and the chief of his bakers were also incarcerated in this same prison. "And the captain of the guard charged Joseph with them, and he served them: and they continued a season in ward."

One morning they looked sad, and Joseph inquired as to the cause of their sadness. They had each dreamed a dream and were troubled for lack of an interpreter. "And Joseph said unto them, Do not interpretations belong to God? tell me them, I pray you" (Gen. 40:8b). They told him their dreams and he interpreted them with God-given accuracy. The butler's dream meant that in three days he would be restored to his former position. The baker's dream, in spite of its apparent similarity, meant that in three days he would be hanged and the birds would eat of his flesh. It all happened precisely as Joseph had interpreted.

Now Joseph had requested of the butler that when he was restored to his former office, he should remember him to Pharaoh, hoping that he too might be released. We can visualize Joseph's hopeful anticipation for several days, or weeks—followed by two full years of disappointment. The butler, when it went well with him, forgot about Joseph. How ungrateful!

Many people forget about Jesus as long as things go well for them. Then when trouble strikes they call on Him for help. Am I (are you) a forgetful *butler* today? Our destiny depends on remembering Jesus as our hope of salvation!

Part Two: Both Obtained Excellent Glory

"And it came to pass at the end of two full years, that Pharaoh dreamed: and, behold, he stood by the river. And, behold, there came up out of the river seven well favoured kine and fatfleshed; and they fed in a meadow. And, behold, seven other kine came up after them out of the river, ill favoured and leanfleshed; and stood by the *other* kine upon the brink of the river. And the ill favoured and leanfleshed kine did eat up the seven well favoured and fat kine. So Pharaoh awoke. And he slept and dreamed the second time: and, behold, seven ears of corn came up upon one stalk, rank and good. And, behold, seven thin ears and blasted with the east wind sprung up after them. And the seven thin ears devoured the seven rank and full ears. And Pharaoh awoke, and, behold, *it was* a dream" (Gen. 41:1-7).

God was working, and Pharaoh was troubled. "He sent and called for all the magicians of Egypt, and all the wise men thereof," but none of them could interpret his dreams. Then the butler remembered Joseph, and with a guilty conscience he confessed his faults [Luther's German translation says, *sins*].

Joseph, the man of the hour, was brought "hastily out of the dungeon." Of interpretation he humbly confessed, "It is not in me: God shall give Pharaoh an answer of peace." Pharaoh told his dreams, the Lord revealed the interpretation, and Joseph said, "God hath showed Pharaoh what he is about to do." In recognition of Joseph's wisdom and ability, Pharaoh made him second in command over all Egypt.

In a few short hours, at age thirty, Joseph rose from a lowly prisoner to the exalted governor of all Egypt. Throughout the seven years of overflowing plenty he supervised the storage of an immeasurable volume of corn (symbolic of "the unsearchable riches of Christ"–Eph. 3:8). In the seven years of famine he supervised the distribution of the corn. "And all countries came into Egypt to Joseph for to buy corn; because that the famine was so sore in all lands" (Gen. 41:57).

Joseph was a human foreshadow of Jesus Christ, who after eighteen silent years, began His earthly ministry, also at age thirty. But Jesus, instead of opening earthly storehouses, opened the windows of heaven, fed five thousand men with five loaves and two fishes, and had twelve basketsful of fragments left over (Mt. 14:17-21). The Substance (Antitype–the person or thing foreshadowed) is always superior to the shadow! "For in him [in Christ Jesus] dwelleth all the fullness of the Godhead bodily" (Col. 2:9).

Nor did Jesus rise merely from an earthly prison to a temporary throne, but from literal death in a tomb to an endless universal reign. "And the government shall be upon his shoulder: and . . . of the increase of his government and peace there shall be no end, upon the throne of David, and upon his kingdom, to order it, and to establish it with judgment and with justice from henceforth even for ever" (Isa. 9:6, 7). He is "KING OF KINGS AND LORD OF LORDS" (Rev. 19:16).

Joseph's ten brothers came down to Egypt to buy corn. Joseph knew them, but they did not know him. With not a word from *home* for twenty-one years, Joseph must have been chock-full of questions. To learn all he could about their present attitudes and family affairs, without revealing his own identity, he questioned them through an interpreter. Treating them as though they were spies, "he put them all together into ward three days." Did he have a secret means of listening to their conversations during that time? What a fruitful source of information that could have been! By the third day Joseph had his strategy planned. Keeping Simeon as a hostage, he released the others to take food to their families, demanding that the next time they must bring Benjamin.

Furthermore, Joseph commanded his servants "to fill their sacks with corn, and to restore every man's money into his sack, and to give them provision for the way." Enroute home one discovered his money in the mouth of his sack. The others found theirs deeper down when they emptied their bags at home. All were alarmed, but it foreshadowed God's Messianic plan: "Come ye, buy, and eat; yea, come, buy wine and milk without money and without price" (Isa. 55:1b). Salvation through Christ cannot be bought with money!

After a while the need for more corn pressed upon them. Jacob was very reluctant to send Benjamin with them, but his sons knew that unless they brought Benjamin they could buy no corn. Judah committed himself to be surety for him, and to bear the blame for ever if he did not bring Benjamin again and set him before Jacob.

"And their father Israel said unto them, If *it must be* so now, do this; take of the best fruits in the land in your vessels, and carry down the man a present, a little balm, and a little honey, spices, and myrrh, nuts, and almonds: and take double money in your hand; and the money that was brought again in the mouth of your sacks, carry *it* again in your hand; peradventure it *was* an oversight: take also your brother, and arise, go again unto the man: and God Almighty give you mercy before the man, that he may send away your other brother, and Benjamin. If I be bereaved *of my children,* I am bereaved" (Gen. 43:11-14).

We cannot use space for all that transpired when they met again with Joseph: their anxieties and fears when they were brought into Joseph's house, how they ate with him, and the honors bestowed upon Benjamin. Joseph commanded his steward to "fill the men's sacks with food, as much as they can carry, and put every man's money in his sack's mouth. And put my cup, the silver cup, in the sack's mouth of the youngest" (44:1-2a). The next morning at daylight the eleven sons of Jacob were sent away, loaded with food, rejoicing to all be together and homeward bound.

Joseph was making sure that his brothers did not envy Benjamin like they had envied him. He sent his steward after them to bring back to him the one who had stolen his silver cup. And sure enough, he found the cup in Benjamin's bag! They rent their clothes, and with heavy hearts they all came back to Joseph's house, "and they fell before him on the ground."

Judah (the very one who had suggested selling Joseph) in a touching plea twenty verses long, presented himself as surety for Benjamin. He finished with, "For how shall I go up to my father, and the lad be not with me? lest peradventure I see the evil that shall come on my father"(44:34). The test was completed. They did not envy Benjamin. The time was ripe for them to discover that the man before whom they bowed in fear and anguish, was Joseph whom their father loved so dearly, and whom they, with bitter hatred, had sold into Egypt!

"Then Joseph could not refrain himself before all them that stood by him; and he cried, Cause every man to go out from me. And there stood no man with him, while Joseph made himself known unto his brethren. And he wept aloud: and the Egyptians and the house of Pharaoh heard.

"And Joseph said unto his brethren, I *am* Joseph; doth my father yet live? And his brethren could not answer him; **for they were troubled at his presence.** And Joseph said unto his brethren, Come near to me, I pray you. And they came near. And he said, **I** *am* **Joseph your brother, whom ye sold into Egypt.** Now therefore be not grieved, nor angry with yourselves, that ye sold me hither: for God did send me before you to preserve life" (Gen. 45:1-5).

"They were troubled at his presence" because they recognized that Joseph had the power to do with them what their cruelty to him had deserved. But Joseph assured them of his pardon and his kindness. A touching scene followed.

There again we see a double and marvelous foreshadow of Christ. "He was in the world, and the world was made by him, and the world **knew him not,**" even as Joseph's brothers did not know Joseph. "But Jesus . . . **knew all men** [better than Joseph knew his brothers] and needed not that any should testify of man: for he knew what was in man" (John 2:24, 25). "He came unto his own, and his own received him not. But as many as received him, to them gave he power to become the sons of God, even to them that believe on his name" (John 1:11-12).

The Bible speaks of a time when Jesus will make Himself known to **His brethren** in the flesh, and they will be troubled by His presence. Like Joseph, He "will pour upon the house of David, and upon the inhabitants of Jerusalem, the spirit of grace and of supplications: and they shall look upon me [Christ] whom they have pierced, and they shall mourn for him, as one mourneth for *his* only *son,* and shall be in bitterness for him, as one that is in bitterness for *his* firstborn. In that day there shall be a great mourning in Jerusalem, as the mourning of Hadadrimmon in the valley of Megiddon. . . . " (Zech. 12:10-14).

This is by no means an exhaustive study of Joseph, but I trust it may be enough to help us appreciate his prominent role in Holy Writ. Bear in mind that all types only foreshadow an antitype, which most often is Jesus Christ. The Substance is always superior to the shadow. The purpose of this study is to help us see Christ more clearly in the Old Testament. Joseph, more than any other character, typified Jesus' suffering in the flesh, climaxed by His future reign and glory.

> **"Looking** unto Jesus the author and finisher of *our* faith; who for the joy that was set before him **endured the cross, despising the shame, and is set down at the right hand of the throne of God** (Heb. 12:2).

Summary of Major Highlights

Joseph, Jacob's eleventh son, was given the birthright by his father (Gen. 49:3-4; 1 Chron. 5:1-2). Jesus, by His Father, is "appointed heir of all things" (Heb. 1:2), "that he might be the firstborn among many brethren" (Rom. 8:29).

"Joseph is . . . a fruitful bough by a well; whose branches run over the wall" (Gen. 49:22). Jesus is the true vine, we are the branches. Without Him we can do nothing (John 15:1-7).

Joseph, at the suggestion of his brother Judah, was sold for twenty pieces of silver. Jesus, by the treachery of His disciple Judas Iscariot, was betrayed (sold) for thirty pieces of silver.

Joseph was sent into Egypt to save lives "by a great deliverance." Jesus "delivered us from so great a death, and doth deliver: in whom we trust that he will yet deliver us" (2 Cor. 1:10).

Joseph said, "God did send me before you to *preserve* life." But "God sent his only begotten Son into the world [to **give** life], that we might live through him" (1 John 4:9).

Joseph bought all the people of Egypt for Pharaoh (Gen. 47:13-23a). Jesus bought with His own blood all those who trust in Him (Acts 20:28; 1 Cor. 6:19, 20).

Joseph, in a Christlike way, freely forgave his brothers. That settled the account between him and his brothers, but only Christ could settle the account between them and God.

Joseph told his brothers that he would nourish them in Egypt (Gen. 45:11). Jesus said, "I am the living bread . . . which I will give for the life of the world" (John 6:51).

Joseph's position in Egypt made the best of the land (Gen. 47:6) available for his family. Jesus' position in heaven enables all faithful believers to be joint-heirs with Christ (Rom. 8:17).

Joseph gave them seed with which to sow the land (47:23b). God through Christ "ministereth seed to the sower, . . . bread for your food, and [will] multiply your seed sown, . . ."(2 Cor. 9:10).

Ada Habershon, in *The Study of the Types,* lists 129 similarities between Joseph and Jesus. Joseph may have typified Christ in a hundred different ways, but only Christ can take away sin.

22
SEEING CHRIST TYPIFIED IN MOSES
Foreshadowing Christ Incarnate Ministering in the Flesh

Moses was born at the time of Pharaoh's order that all Hebrew male babies be cast into the river (Ex. 1:22). But God intervened. Moses was saved alive and became a royal prince in Egypt. When Jesus was born, Herod undertook to slay all the children two years old and under, in and around Bethlehem (Mt. 2:13-16). But God informed Joseph to take the Baby Jesus and flee into Egypt, where Jesus too was saved alive, and remains a Prince in the House of David.

Moses, at age forty, sacrificed his adopted royalty. He chose "to suffer affliction with the people of God, . . . esteeming the reproach of Christ greater riches than the treasures of Egypt" (Heb. 11:25-26). In so doing he beautifully foreshadowed Jesus, "who, being in the form of God, . . . took upon him the form of a servant, . . . humbled himself, and became obedient unto death, even the death of the cross" (Phil. 2:6-8).

For forty years "Moses fled from the face of Pharaoh, and dwelt in the land of Midian." As a servant and shepherd, he "kept the flock of Jethro his father-in-law, the priest of Midian." For thirty-three years Jesus gave up His prerogatives as God's equal in heaven, and voluntarily condescended lower than Moses ever did. He was born in a lowly stable in Bethlehem. As a child He fled for his life as a refugee, to the land of Moses' birth. Later He returned and grew to manhood in the despised little village of Nazareth. He dwelt on earth and kept His Father's flock (John 17:12), who would become the church "which he hath purchased with his own blood" (Acts 20:28).

"And the Lord spake unto Moses face to face, as a man speaketh unto his friend" (Ex. 33:11). Through Moses, God wrought many miracles in Egypt before Pharaoh relinquished his grip on the Israelites. But that is only a shadow of how Jesus continues to deliver captives of Satan in every era: past, present, and future. Moses delivered the Israelites from bondage to Pharaoh in Egypt, but Jesus delivers faithful believers world-wide and from age to age from their bondage to Satan. However beautiful a type may be, the Substance (or Antitype) always outshines the shadow.

Moses was a great intercessor. The Israelites were a stiff-necked people, repeatedly testing the patience of Moses. Four times God threatened to utterly destroy them. Twice He offered to consume them and make of Moses "a great nation" (Ex. 32:10), "a greater nation and mightier than they" (Nu. 14:12). Twice more He told Moses and Aaron to separate themselves from the congregation "that I may consume them in a moment" (Nu. 16:21, 45). Each time Moses interceded mightily:

> "And Moses besought the LORD his God, and said, LORD, why doth thy wrath wax hot against thy people, which thou hast brought forth out of the land of Egypt with great power and with a mighty hand? Wherefore should the Egyptians speak, and say, For mischief did he bring them out, to slay them in the mountains, and to consume them from the face of the earth?
>
> "Turn from thy fierce wrath, and repent of this evil against thy people. Remember Abraham, Isaac, and Israel, thy servants, to whom thou swarest by thine own self, and saidst unto them, I will multiply your seed as the stars of heaven, and all this land that I have spoken of will I give unto your seed, and they shall inherit *it* for ever. And the LORD repented of the evil which he thought to do unto his people" (Ex. 32:11-14).
>
> "And Moses said unto the LORD, Then the Egyptians shall hear *it*, (for thou broughtest up this people in thy might from among them;) and they will tell *it* to the inhabitants of this land:

for they have heard that thou LORD *art* among this people, that thou LORD are seen face to face, and *that* thy cloud standeth over them, and *that* thou goest before them, by day time in a pillar of a cloud, and in a pillar of fire by night.

"Now *if* thou shalt kill *all* this people as one man, then the nations which have heard the fame of thee will speak saying, Because the LORD was not able to bring this people into the land which he sware unto them, therefore he hath slain them in the wilderness. And now, I beseech thee, let the power of my LORD be great, according as thou hast spoken, saying, The LORD *is* longsuffering, and of great mercy, forgiving iniquity and trans-gression, and by no means clearing *the guilty*, visiting the iniq-uity of the fathers upon the children unto the third and fourth *generation*. Pardon, I beseech thee, the iniquity of this people according unto the greatness of thy mercy, and as thou hast for-given this people, from Egypt even until now" (Nu. 14:13-19).

The most important promise God made to Moses was that of a Successor **like unto** [but greater than] Moses. He said,

I will raise them up a Prophet from among their brethren, **like unto thee**, and will put my words in his mouth; and he shall speak unto them all that I shall command him. And it shall come to pass, *that* whosoever will not hearken unto my words which he shall speak in my name, I will require *it* of him" (Dt. 18:18-19).

God distinctly likened Moses unto Christ. The New Testament, however, indicates that Christ not only surpasses but supersedes Moses. "For the law was given by Moses, but grace and truth came by Jesus Christ" (John 1:17). Six times in Matthew 5:21-48 Jesus raised Mosaic standards to new and higher levels.

Their comparison and Christ's preeminence are both emphasized in the Book of Hebrews:

"Wherefore, holy brethren, partakers of the heavenly call-ing, consider the Apostle and High Priest of our profession, Christ Jesus; who was faithful to him that appointed him, as also Moses *was faithful* in all his house.

"For this *man* was counted **worthy of more glory** than Moses, inasmuch as he who hath builded the house hath more honour than the house. For every house is builded by some *man*; but he that built all things *is* God. And Moses verily *was* faithful in all his house, as a servant, for a testimony of those things which were to be spoken after; but Christ as a son over his own house; whose house are we, if we hold fast the confidence and the rejoicing of the hope firm unto the end" (3:1-6).

". . . Moses was admonished of God when he was about to make the tabernacle: for, See, saith he, *that* thou make all things according to the **pattern** showed to thee in the mount. But now hath [Christ] obtained a **more excellent ministry**, by how much also he is the mediator of a **better covenant**, which was established upon **better promises**.

"For if that first *covenant* had been faultless, then should no place have been sought for the second. For finding fault with them, he saith, Behold, the days come, saith the Lord, when I will make a **new covenant** with the house of Israel and with the house of Judah: not according to the covenant that I made with their fathers in the day when I took them by the hand to lead them out of the land of Egypt; because they continued not in my covenant, and I regarded them not, saith the Lord" (8:5-9).

"In that he saith, A **new** *covenant*, he hath made the first old. Now that which decayeth and waxeth old *is* ready to vanish away" (8:13).

For when Moses had spoken every precept to all the people according to the law, he took the blood of calves and of goats, with water, and scarlet wool, and hyssop, and sprinkled both the book, and all the people, saying, This *is* the blood of the testament which God hath enjoined unto you" (9:19-20).

"*It was* therefore necessary that the patterns of things in the heavens should be purified with these; but the heavenly things themselves with **better sacrifices** than these. For Christ is not entered into the holy places made with hands, *which are* the **figures** of the true; but into heaven itself, now to appear in the presence of God for us" (9:23-24).

"For the law having a **shadow** of good things to come, *and* not the very image of the things, can never with those sacrifices which they offered year by year continually make the comers thereunto perfect" (10:1).

"For *it is* not possible that the blood of bulls and of goats should take away sins. Wherefore when [Christ] cometh into the world, he saith, Sacrifice and offering thou wouldest not, but a body hast thou prepared me: in burnt offerings and sacrifices for sin thou hast had no pleasure" (10:4-6).

"Then said he, Lo, I come to do thy will O God. He taketh away the first that he may establish the second. By the which will we are sanctified **through the offering of the body of Jesus Christ once for all**" (10:9-10).

Moses further foreshadowed the ministry of Christ in the following instances:

- Both fasted forty days and nights (Dt. 9:9, 25; Luke 4:2).
- Both confronted and defeated Satan (Ex. 7:11-12; Luke 4:2).
- Both had power over the sea (Ex. 14:21; Mt. 8:26).
- Both fed multitudes of people (Ex. 16:35; Nu. 11:31; Mark 6:41-42).
- Both were discredited by their siblings (Nu. 12:1; John 7:3-5).
- Both were famous teachers (Dt. 4:5; Mark 10:1).
- Both were great prophets of God (Dt. 34:10; Luke 7:16).
- Both foretold many future events (Dt. 28, 29, 30; Mt. 24).
- Both were sent to save their own people (Ex. 3:10; Mt. 23:37).
- Both were rejected in their first attempt (Ex. 2:14; John 1:11).
- Both were divinely appointed judges (Ex. 18:13; John 5:22).
- Both were destined to glorious success (Ex. 12-15; Rev. 19:11-16).
- Both had seventy helpers (Nu. 11:16, 17; Luke 10:1).
- Both endured the contradiction of sinners (Nu. 16:2, 3; Heb 12:3).
- Both endured unjust accusations (Nu. 16:12-14; Mt. 9:34).
- Both spoke the Word of God with power (Nu. 16:23-32; Luke 4:32).
- Both encountered bitter envy (Ps. 106:16; Mark 15:10)

- Both established memorials (Ex. 12:14; Luke 22:19).
- Both reappeared after death (Mt. 17:3; Acts 1:3).

Moses, the meekest man on earth (Nu. 12:3), fell in his strongest virtue. He had for forty years endured Israel's murmurings and strife with patience, then *lost it* at the waters of Meribah (Nu. 20:10-13; Dt. 3:23-27). "They angered *him* . . ., so that it went ill with Moses for their sakes: because they provoked his spirit, so that he spake unadvisedly with his lips" (Ps. 106:32-33). And *for our sakes* it went ill with Jesus, the **Great Antitype** of Moses.

Before Moses died, at the age of 120, he blessed Israel tribe by tribe (Dt. 33). Then, alone, he climbed mount Nebo to the top of Pisgah, and the LORD caused him to see all the land, but he could not enter in. No one knows what their last conversation may have been before God put Moses to sleep. Nor has anyone ever found the secret burial plot where God Himself laid the body of Moses to rest (Dt. 34).

Six times the Bible gives Him the honorable title, "Moses the man of God." "And there arose not a prophet since in Israel like unto Moses, whom the LORD knew face to face" (Dt. 34:10).

23

SEEING CHRIST TYPIFIED IN

AARON AND ELEAZAR

Foreshadowing Christ's Earthly Ministry, His Ascension,
His Headship of the Church and Second Coming

I. AARON TYPIFIED CHRIST'S FIRST ADVENT

Aaron, offering thousands of sacrifices, typified Christ's First Advent. There were the twice daily burnt offerings. There were weekly, monthly, and annual sacrifices for the whole congregation to be repeated over and over at regular intervals. In addition to the routine there was a constant flow of special and personal sacrifices for two million people. Every offering prefigured certain aspects of what Christ did for us when He offered Himself—the **Ultimate Sacrifice**.

Christ, in His First Advent, offered the one and only Sacrifice that could take away sin. All the others were symbols of that one sacrifice. They were reminders of man's need, and of the enormous ransom Jesus voluntarily paid. Man needs to be reminded of the terrible cost of sin. The multiple thousands of animals thus sacrificed were merely a shadow—*not even a down-payment*—of what our sins have cost our Savior. In addition to His sacrifice He has already invested six thousand years in our salvation.

Christ's High Priesthood Foreshadowed in Aaron

Aaron's call to the priesthood lacks no certainty (Ex. 4:14-16a; 28:1). When Korah and his men challenged it (Nu. 16:1-19), God reconfirmed Aaron's appointment fourfold.

- The earth opened up and swallowed alive the initiators of the rebellion (16:29-34).
- Fire from the LORD "consumed the two hundred and fifty men that offered incense" (v. 35).
- Fourteen thousand seven hundred murmurers died of the plague (16:41-49).
- Aaron's rod "brought forth buds, and blossomed blossoms, and yielded almonds" (17:1-8).

There is something special about **Aaron and his sons** (a phrase that occurs twenty-nine times in the Old Testament). Earlier priests were alone in their office. All of Aaron's sons were priests by virtue of Aaron's anointing and because they were his sons. Together they typify the priesthood of all true Christians. Jesus Christ "hath made **us** kings and priests unto God" (Rev. 1:5-6; 5:10; 20:6). Christians have "a royal priesthood" (1 Pet. 2:9) by virtue of being born of God (John 1:13).

High priest is a title found only twenty-one times in the Old Testament and fifty-four times in the New. Its use in the Old Testament, the Gospels and Acts may be confined to the Levitical priesthood. But the Book of Hebrews applies that title to Christ eleven times. He is the High Priest of all true believers. No one has access to God except through Christ our High Priest.

Before Aaron and his sons assumed their priestly duties they had a consecration ceremony, repeated each day for seven days. First of all Moses had to wash their bodies daily for seven days. That washing foreshadowed a New Testament imperative— "the washing of regeneration" (Titus 3:5), which only God can do. The LORD had said Moses shall be to Aaron "instead of God" (Ex. 4:16b). Moses was God's proxy, doing physically what only God can do spiritually.

Throughout the seven days of their consecration Moses did everything for them. He washed them, clothed them, did the anointing and all the sacrificing (Ex. 29:1-37; 40:12-16; Lev. 8:1-36). Aaron and his sons were passive, like children who cannot clothe themselves. The only thing they did was to lay their hands on the heads of the bullock for the sin offering, the ram for a burnt offering, and the ram of consecration (Ex. 29:10, 15, 20).

Then Moses slew the animals in their respective order, and did with the blood of each what God had commanded. God said,

> "And ye shall not go out of the door of the tabernacle . . . in seven days, until the days of your consecration be at an end: for seven days shall he [Moses] consecrate you. . . . Therefore shall ye abide at the door of the tabernacle . . . day and night seven days, and keep the charge of the LORD, **that ye die not**: for so I am commanded" (Lev. 8:33, 35).

Not until the eighth day (Lev. 9:1) did Aaron begin to offer the sacrifices. What Moses did each day for seven days symbolized what man cannot do for himself. And having continued the process for seven days suggests that God continues the cleansing and consecrating process for each child of His as long as we abide in Him—even as Aaron and his sons abode in the tabernacle, so must we abide in Christ day and night continually, **that we die not.** God always has to do something **to** us and **for** us before He can freely work **through** us.

Christ's Ascension Typified by Aaron

Aaron, even in his death, typified Christ in His First Coming. When Aaron's time came to die, God said to Moses,

> "Take Aaron and Eleazar his son, and bring them up unto mount Hor: and strip Aaron of his garments, and put them upon Eleazar his son: and Aaron shall be gathered *unto his people,* and shall die there.
>
> "And Moses did as the LORD commanded: and they went up into mount Hor in the sight of all the congregation. And

Moses stripped Aaron of his garments, and put them upon Eleazar his son; and Aaron died there in the top of the mount: and Moses and Eleazar came down from the mount" (Nu. 20:25-28).

We read nothing about Aaron's burial. Evidently that was kept out of the record by design. Aaron ascended Mount Hor in the sight of all the congregation, and disappeared from the record. It beautifully typifies Jesus literally disappearing when He ascended from Mount Olivet back to heaven (Acts 1:9-10).

II. ELEAZAR TYPIFIED CHRIST'S PRESENT MINISTRY AND HIS SECOND COMING

Notice Eleazar coming down from Mount Hor. He bears the same office and wears all the high priestly robes in which Aaron ascended. Eleazar descending in his new role typifies Christ descending in His Second Coming. When Jesus comes again He too will descend bearing a **new and greater role** than He did while living here in the flesh.

For years, while Aaron still lived, Eleazar typified Christ's High Priestly ministry in the present Holy Spirit age. Eleazar was "chief over the chief of the Levites," and had "the oversight of them that keep the charge of the sanctuary" (Nu. 3:32). The Levites typified the New Testament church, and the Tabernacle typified Christ and His church on earth. (Described in the author's other book, *Seeing Christ in the Tabernacle*).

To Eleazar pertained "the oil for the light [denoting the Holy Spirit age], and the sweet incense [prayers of the saints], and the daily meat offering [uniform perfection of Jesus' life and character], and the anointing oil [divine unction], *and* the oversight of all the tabernacle [church of Christ on earth], and of all that therein *is,* in the sanctuary, and in the vessels thereof" (Nu. 4:16).

All that was while Aaron still lived. Eleazar, as the oldest survivor of Aaron's sons, was in line to be the second high priest. His duties already typified Christ as Head of the Church from His position in heaven in the present Holy Spirit age.

But Eleazar ascended Mount Hor in white linen garments as *an assistant priest.* He was not yet eligible to wear the robe of blue; nor the ephod, the curious girdle, and the breast plate of judgment (the last three interwoven with gold). Nor did he wear the mitre with the plate of gold (Ex. 28:4-8, 36). All that changed on Mount Hor, depicting the end time promotion of Jesus.

Eleazar descended Mount Hor endued with the highest priestly office the Mosaic Law could offer. When Christ returns again from heaven He will be endued with the highest offices that ever descended upon this earth. His Priesthood and His Kingdom will both be universal and insuperable. He will come with royal splendor, to assume with invincible power all the offices that pertain to the Lord of Glory and King of kings, for **"Jesus Christ is Lord, to the glory of God the Father"** (Phil. 2:11).

24

SEEING CHRIST TYPIFIED IN TWO JOSHUAS

Joshua the son of Nun (Exodus through Judges)
Joshua the son of Josedech (Haggai and Zechariah)

These two Joshuas lived nearly a thousand years apart, but each in his own role foreshadowed Christ. The name Jehoshua meant *Jehovah saves,* or *Jehovah is Salvation* (Nu. 13:16). The name itself denotes a foreshadow of Jesus. The shortened form (Joshua) still means the same, which in Greek translates to *Jesus.* "And thou shalt call his name JESUS: for *he shall save his people from their sins*" (Mt. 1:21).

I. JOSHUA THE SON OF NUN

Joshua the son of Nun, of the tribe of Ephraim, first comes on the scene in Exodus 17:9-16. Israel was enjoying tremendous blessings from the smitten Rock of Horeb. Their chiding with Moses had just been silenced by the gushing forth of water from the smitten Rock.

"**Then came Amalek,** and fought with Israel in Rephidim. And Moses said unto **Joshua,** Choose us out men, and go out, fight with Amalek: to morrow I will stand on the top of the hill with the rod of God in mine hand.

"So **Joshua** did as Moses had said to him, and fought with Amalek: and Moses, Aaron, and Hur went up to the top of the hill. And it came to pass, when Moses held up his hand, that

Israel prevailed: and when he let down his hand, Amalek prevailed.

"But Moses' hands *were* heavy; and they took a stone, and put *it* under him, and he sat thereon; and Aaron and Hur stayed up his hands, the one on the one side, and the other on the other side; and his hands were steady until the going down of the sun. And **Joshua** discomfited Amalek and his people with the edge of the sword" (Ex. 17:8-13).

This was the first time Israel needed to fight. In Moses' encounters with Pharaoh, God did everything for them. When they were trapped with the Red Sea in their path, God parted the waters, took Israel through on dry ground, and drowned the Egyptians behind them. When they feared death from lack of water, God opened the Rock in Horeb, and supplied water in abundance. But when Amalek came, Israel had to participate in the fight.

Our *Joshua* to Control Our *Amalek*

"And the LORD said unto Moses, Write this *for* a memorial in a book, and rehearse *it* in the ears of **Joshua**: for I will utterly put out the remembrance of Amalek from under heaven. And Moses built an altar, and called the name of it **Jehovah-nissi**: for he said, Because the LORD hath sworn *that* the LORD *will have* war with Amalek from generation to generation" (Ex. 17:14-16).

Amalek was a grandson of Esau (Gen. 36:12). Both typify natural (unregenerate) man. God is at war with our *Amalek* (carnal nature), and He expects us to participate in the fight. Jesus (our *Joshua*—our *Jehovah-nissi*) will help us, but we must cooperate and do our part.

God did not back off, but He made victory contingent upon cooperation from Israel. He also made them responsible for continued cooperation in the future. The Lord did not annihilate Amalek, just as He does not eradicate the flesh of a Christian. But He warned Israel not to forget that eventually they are to "blot out the remembrance of Amalek " (Dt. 25:17-19), just as we are to "mortify [put to death] the deeds of the body" (Rom. 8:13; Col. 3:5). "Flesh and blood cannot inherit the kingdom of God" (1 Cor. 15:50). "Ye **must** be born again" (John 3:7).

Joshua the Servant of Moses

Next we see Joshua as Moses' minister (Ex. 24:13), accompanying Moses and seventy elders part way up Mount Sinai (24:1-2). We are not sure where Joshua was during the forty days that Moses alone communed with God in the glory cloud. But I suspect that, as "the servant of Moses," he may have stayed close by, keeping watch in prayer. Apparently he alone descended with Moses. When they heard Israel singing and dancing around the golden calf, Joshua mistook it for the noise of war in the camp" (Ex. 32:17). That suggests his absence from the camp during those forty days.

Joshua Moses' Successor

"And the LORD said unto Moses, Take thee Joshua the son of Nun, a man in whom *is* the spirit, and lay thine hand upon him; and set him before Eleazar the priest, and before all the congregation; and give him a charge in their sight" (Nu. 27:18-19).

"And Joshua the son of Nun was full of the spirit of wisdom; for Moses had laid his hands upon him: and the children of Israel hearkened unto him, and did as the LORD commanded Moses" (Dt. 34:9).

The time had come when "Moses the man of God" needed to be replaced with a divinely chosen successor. Moses had typified Christ as God's chosen Instructor and Prophet (Dt. 18:15, 18). Through him God gave the Ten Commandments and the Mosaic Law to teach how man should live. "This do, and thou shalt live" (Luke 10:28).

The Law was good, but fallen man is incapable of living by the Law. Every man needs a personal Savior. "Wherefore the law was our school-master [disciplinarian, so the German] to bring us unto Christ, that we might be justified by faith" (Gal. 3:24). So God chose Joshua, a man whose name means *Jehovah saves*. As Moses represented the Law, so Joshua represented the Savior. "For the law was given by Moses, but grace and truth came by Jesus Christ" (John 1:17).

Moses taught them the way and led them all the way through the wilderness. But it took Joshua (typifying our Jehovah Savior) to bring Israel over the Jordan, and divide unto them the promised inheritance.

> "And the people served the LORD all the days of Joshua, and all the days of the elders that outlived Joshua, who had seen all the great works of the LORD, that he did for Israel. And Joshua, the son of Nun, the servant of the LORD, died, *being* an hundred and ten years old" (Judges 2:7-8).

II. JOSHUA THE SON OF JOSEDECH

Some nine hundred years later *(after the Babylonian captivity)* we find Joshua the son of Josedech. He was high priest at Jerusalem while they were rebuilding the temple. His name appears five times in Haggai chapters one and two, and six times in Zechariah chapters three and six. (Known as Jeshua the son of Jozadak in Ezra and Nehemiah, where he appears twice as often.)

We are confining our observations of this man to the visions of Zechariah, where the Lord used him in a unique way to foreshadow Jesus Christ. We will let Zechariah tell the story, and let the Lord give the basic interpretation by His written Word.

> "And he showed me Joshua the high priest standing before the angel of the LORD, and Satan standing at his right hand to resist him. And the LORD said unto Satan, The LORD rebuke thee, O Satan; even the LORD that hath chosen Jerusalem rebuke thee: *is* not this a brand plucked out of the fire?
>
> "Now Joshua was clothed with filthy garments, and stood before the angel. And he answered and spake unto those that stood before him, saying, Take away the filthy garments from him. And unto him he said, Behold, I have caused thine iniquity to pass from thee, and I will clothe thee with change of raiment" (Zech. 3:1-4).

In the above verses Joshua the high priest in his filthy garments symbolized the corruption of the nation of Israel, as
well as of Jerusalem and their priests, of which Joshua was
one. Satan stood there at his right hand to resist, or accuse
him. But the LORD rebuked Satan, suggesting that this is a
brand plucked out of the fire, and proceeded to illustrate what
He is going to do with this brand. Then He introduced the
BRANCH (the Lord Jesus Christ), and Satan's mouth was
stopped.

> "And I said, Let them set a fair mitre upon his head. So they
> set a fair mitre upon his head, and clothed him with garments.
> And the angel of the LORD stood by. And the angel of the
> LORD protested unto Joshua, saying, Thus saith the LORD of
> hosts; If thou wilt walk in my ways, and if thou wilt keep my
> charge, then thou shalt also judge my house, and shalt also keep
> my courts, and I will give thee places to walk among these that
> stand by.
>
> "Hear now, O Joshua the high priest, thou, and thy fellows
> that sit before thee: for they *are* men wondered at: for, behold, I
> will bring forth my servant the BRANCH. For behold the stone
> that I have laid before Joshua; upon one stone *shall be* seven
> eyes: behold, I will engrave the graving thereof, saith the LORD
> of hosts, and I will **remove the iniquity of that land in one day**.
> In that day, saith the LORD of hosts, shall ye call every man his
> neighbour under the vine and under the fig tree" (Zech. 3:5-10).

Chapter six shows a symbolic coronation of Joshua, typifying The BRANCH introduced in chapter three, and
describes what He will do. Joshua was a high priest but he
was not a king.

> "And the word of the LORD came unto me, saying, Take of
> *them of* the captivity, *even* of Heldai, of Tobijah, and of Jedaiah,
> which are come from Babylon, and come thou the same day, and
> go into the house of Josiah the son of Zephaniah; Then take sil-
> ver and gold, and make crowns, and set *them* upon the head of
> Joshua the son of Josedech, the high priest; and speak unto him,
> saying, Thus speaketh the LORD of hosts, saying, Behold the
> man whose name *is* The BRANCH; and he shall grow up out of

his place, and he shall build the temple of the LORD: even he shall build the temple of the LORD; and he shall bear the glory, and shall sit and rule upon his throne; and he [The Branch] shall be **a priest upon his throne:** and the counsel of peace shall be between them both.

"And the crowns shall be to Helem, and to Tobijah, and to Jedaiah, and to Hen the son of Zephaniah, for a memorial in the temple of the LORD. And they *that are* far off shall come and build in the temple of the LORD, and ye shall know that the LORD of hosts hath sent me unto you. And *this* shall come to pass, if ye will diligently obey the voice of the LORD your God" (Zech. 6:9-15).

The crowning described above did not make Joshua a king. He was a priest, which had to be of the tribe of Levi. Their kings had to be of the tribe of Judah. For an Israelite king to invade the priest's office brought dire consequences (1 Sam.13:9-14; 2 Chron. 26:16-21). And for a Levitical priest to usurp the throne was unthinkable. Only Melchizedek, a hundred and forty years before Levi or Judah were born, typified Christ as king and priest by actually holding both offices. Joshua did not wear those crowns. They were to be kept for a memorial in the temple of the Lord (Zech. 6:14, 15).

For more about *The Branch*, See **The Servant Branch** Pg.181

25

SEEING CHRIST TYPIFIED IN BOAZ

Depicting the Riches of His Grace for both Jews and Gentiles

Moab was not in good standing with the Lord (Nu. 21:29). They hired Balaam to curse Israel, but God overruled (Nu. 22–24). When Balaam could not curse them, they lured Israel to the sacrifices of their gods. "Israel joined himself unto Baal-peor: and the anger of the Lord was kindled against Israel (25:1-3). As a result 24,000 Israelites died in the plague. And God said, "An Ammonite or Moabite shall not enter into the congregation of the LORD; . . . for ever" (Dt. 23:3).

Centuries later, during one of the seven cycles of apostasy recorded in the Book of Judges, there was a famine in the land of Israel (a result of apostasy). Elimelech (which means *God is King*) and Naomi (which means *pleasant)*, with their two sons, Chilion and Mahlon, departed from Bethlehem (*house of bread*), and went (of all places) "into the country of Moab, and continued there . . . about ten years" (Ruth 1:1-4). Their sojourn in Moab typified Israel's Dispersion among the Gentiles. Elimelech and both sons died in Moab, leaving Naomi to typify the remnant of dispersed Israel.

Naomi "heard in the country of Moab how that the LORD had visited his people [Israel] in giving them bread" (1:6). But she, in her widowhood, was still pining away in Moab (*like Israel destitute in the Dispersion*). So Naomi, with her daughter-in-law Ruth, returned to Bethlehem.

143

> "All the city was moved about them, and they said, Is this
> Naomi And she said unto them, Call me not Naomi, call me
> Mara: for the Almighty hath dealt very bitterly with me. I went
> out full, and the LORD hath brought me home again empty: why
> then call ye me Naomi, seeing the LORD hath testified against
> me, and the **Almighty** hath afflicted me" (Ruth 1:19-21).

That sounds quite negative, but it is not the end of the
story. The affliction undoubtedly was a long-term result of
Israel's apostasy. But now the **Almighty** (Shaddai) brought
her back to Bethlehem (house of bread). There He restored
both Naomi (*the remnant of Israel*) and Ruth (the Moabitess)
through the good graces of Boaz (a manifold type of Jesus
Christ).

What about God's verdict that a Moabite shall not enter
into the congregation of the LORD (Dt. 23:3)? That commandment, apparently, did not apply to women. Often when
Israel encountered an enemy in battle, they were to "smite
every male thereof with the edge of the sword: but the women
and the little ones, . . . shalt thou take unto thyself [as a spoil]"
(Dt. 20:13-15). Compare also Numbers 31:7-18.

Ruth's situation, however, was a special revelation of
God's marvelous grace, available only through faith in Christ.
All of us were born sinners by nature. But by faith in Christ
our enmity toward God is transformed into adoption. Ruth
had been a Moabite by birth. But she thoroughly denounced
her pagan heritage and embraced the saving faith that still lin-
gered dimly in her mother-in-law. To Naomi she voiced her
decision, and lived up to her commitment.

> "Entreat me not to leave thee, *or* to return from following
> after thee: for whither thou goest, I will go; and where thou
> lodgest, I will lodge: thy people *shall be* my people, and thy God
> my God: where thou diest, will I die, and there will I be buried:
> the LORD do so to me, and more also, *if ought* but death part thee
> and me" (Ruth 1:16-17).

Ruth was sincere and steadfast in her decision. God knew
her heart and provided for her a legal adoption into the

household of faith, by virtue of her Redeemer, Jesus Christ. Boaz was a near kinsman and a beautiful foreshadow of Christ. Both Boaz and Christ are:

- Israelites from Bethlehem (Ruth 2:4; Mt. 2:1)
- near kinsmen of Naomi (2:1, 3, 20; Jn. 4:22b)
- mighty men of wealth (2:1; Heb. 1:2)
- owners of the field (2:3; Jn. 4:35)
- masters of the harvest (2-9; Lu.10:2; Jn. 4:35)
- channels of grace to strangers (2:10-11; 2 Cor. 8:9)
- comforters of the needy (2:12-13; Jn. 14:18)
- suppliers of every need (2:14-17; Phil. 4:19)
- gracious givers of rest (3:1; Mt. 11:28)
- redeemers of their inheritance (4:4-9; Acts 20:32)
- purchasers of a Gentile bride (4:10; Acts 20:28)
- restorers of life (4:15; Acts 3:20-21)
- nourishers of old age (4:15; Isa. 46:3, 4; Mal. 3:6)

It was the duty of near kinsmen to attend to the needs of widows. And when a man died childless, his brother was to marry his widow, and their first son was to be reckoned as the seed of her first husband, "that his name be not put out of Israel" (Dt. 25:5-10). Naomi and Ruth had one kinsman nearer than Boaz, but he declined to marry Ruth, lest he mar his own inheritance (Ruth 4:6). Therefore Boaz, the redeemer of their inheritance, "bought all that was Elimelech's, and all that was Chilion's and Mahlon's at the hand of Naomi" (4:9)

Boaz said, "Moreover Ruth the Moabitess . . . have I purchased to be my wife" (Ruth 4:10). Thus, by God's grace, Ruth became the wife of Boaz and gave birth to a son whom they named Obed. Obed begat Jesse and Jesse begat David.

"And the women said unto Naomi, Blessed *be* the LORD, which hath not left thee this day without a **kinsman**, that his name may be famous in Israel. *A*nd he shall be unto thee a **restorer of *thy* life**, and a **nourisher of thine old age**: for thy daughter in law, which loveth thee, which is better to thee than seven sons, hath borne him. And Naomi took the child, and laid it in her bosom, and became nurse unto it" (Ruth 4:14-16).

Ruth, a great-grandmother to King David, has the honor of being one of the five women named in the genealogy of Jesus (Mt. 1:5). What a beautiful portrait of divine redemption!

Boaz did not marry Naomi, but she was fully accepted as an important member of the home. Her every need was provided for and supplied. What Boaz became to Naomi, foreshadows what Christ is to the Jews today. Christ (like Boaz) purchased a Gentile Bride (Acts 20:28), but He has not cast away His People (Rom. 11:1). When Jews (as well as Gentiles) receive Jesus Christ into their heart (like Naomi embraced the child that Ruth had borne), He becomes their Savior as well.

"Now if the fall of them *be* the riches of the world, and the diminishing of them the riches of the Gentiles; how much more their fulness? For I speak to you Gentiles, inasmuch as I am the apostle of the Gentiles, I magnify mine office: if by any means I may provoke to emulation *them which are* my flesh, and might save some of them. For if the casting away of them *be* the reconciling of the world, what *shall* the receiving *of them be,* but life from the dead?" (Rom. 11:12-15).

"For if thou wert cut out of the olive tree which is wild by nature, and wert grafted contrary to nature into a good olive tree: how much more shall these, which be the natural *branches,* be grafted into their own olive tree? For I would not, brethren, that ye should be ignorant of this mystery, lest ye should be wise in your own conceits; that blindness in part is happened to Israel, until the fulness of the Gentiles be come in" (Rom. 11:24-25).

"O the depth of the riches both of the wisdom and knowledge of God! how unsearchable *are* his judgments, and his ways past finding out!" (Rom. 11:33).

26
SEEING CHRIST TYPIFIED IN SAMUEL
Foreshadowing Christ Incarnate Ministering in the Flesh

Melchizedek typified Christ as Priest and King. David typified Him as King and Prophet. But Samuel typified Him as Prophet, Priest, and Judge. I know of no other man who prefigured Christ in those three offices. And I know of no other Bible character named Samuel. Yet his name occurs 142 times in the Bible.

Scores of Bible names begin or end with El, the shortest name for God. I know of none that have it elsewhere in the name. Those two letters in a proper noun usually denote the Mighty El, or God Almighty.

Samuel's father, Elkanah, had two wives, Hannah and Penninah. Penninah had both sons and daughters, but Hannah had no children. Every year they went to Shiloh to worship and sacrifice to the Lord. Penninah kept taunting Hannah about being childless, just to provoke her. Finally, after eating at Shiloh, Hannah went into the house of the Lord in bitterness of soul. There she prayed desperately for a son, committing herself to give him to the Lord all his life.

> "And she vowed a vow, and said, O LORD of hosts, if thou wilt indeed look on the affliction of thine handmaid, and remember me, and not forget thine handmaid, but wilt give unto thine handmaid a man child, then I will give him unto the LORD all the days of his life, and there shall no razor come upon his head" (1 Sam. 1:11).

The LORD answered her prayer with a healthy son, whom she named Samuel, because she had **asked him of the Lord.**   When she had "weaned him" (perhaps weaned of childish ways, and trained for adolescent responsibilities) she brought him to Eli the priest and left him there.

> "But Samuel ministered before the LORD, *being* a child, girded with a linen ephod. Moreover his mother made him a little coat, and brought *it* to him from year to year, when she came up with her husband to offer the yearly sacrifice" (1 Sam. 2:18-19).

Imagine all the love Hannah sewed into those coats year after year! She may have measured a boy his age to calculate Samuel's growth. She had committed him to the LORD, resting assured that the LORD will guard him with special care. He did.

> "And Eli blessed Elkanah and his wife, and said, The LORD give thee seed of this woman for the loan which is lent to the LORD. And they went unto their own home. And the LORD visited Hannah, so that she conceived, and bare three sons and two daughters. And the child Samuel grew before the LORD" (1 Sam. 2:20-21).

> "And the child Samuel grew on, and was in favour both with the LORD, and also with men" (1 Sam. 2:26). Thus typifying Jesus.

> "And Jesus increased in wisdom and stature, and in favour with God and man" (Luke 2:52).

> "And Samuel grew, and the LORD was with him, and **did let none of his words fall to the ground**. And all Israel from Dan even to Beersheba knew that Samuel *was* established *to be* a **prophet of the LORD**. And the LORD appeared again in Shiloh: for the LORD revealed himself to Samuel in Shiloh by the word of the LORD" (1 Sam. 3:19-21). **He was their Prophet.**

Samuel spoke to all the house of Israel, telling them to put away their strange gods and to serve God only. He called them together to Mizpeh, "and Samuel judged the children of Israel in Mizpeh" (1 Sam. 7:6c).

> "And Samuel took a sucking lamb, and offered *it for* a burnt offering wholly unto the LORD: and Samuel cried unto the LORD for Israel; and the LORD heard him. And as Samuel was offering up the burnt offering, the Philistines drew near to battle against Israel: but the LORD thundered with a great thunder on that day upon the Philistines, and discomfited them; and they were smitten before Israel" (1 Sam. 7:9-10). **He was their priest.**

> "So the Philistines were subdued, and they came no more into the coast of Israel: and the hand of the LORD was against the Philistines all the days of Samuel" (7:13).

> "And Samuel judged Israel all the days of his life" (7:15).
He was their judge.

When Samuel was old he made his sons judges over Israel. That was a mistake, for "his sons walked not in his ways." Therefore the people requested to have a king "like all the nations." That displeased Samuel, but the Lord told him to give them a king (8:1-9).

God chose the man (1 Sam. 9:15-17), and Samuel anointed him privately (10:1). Later he called a public meeting, and revealed by lot that God had chosen Saul (10:17-25). Their kings were to be from the tribe of Judah (Gen. 49:10). But God, possibly for some typological reason, chose Saul of the tribe of Benjamin to be their first king.

In a few short years Saul violated his assignment by invading the priesthood (13:8-13). Therefore God sought a young man (evidently a teenager) who would eventually replace Saul (13:14).

Samuel commissioned Saul to destroy the Amalekites, man and beast (1 Sam. 15:1-3) as God had decreed (Ex. 17:14, 16). Saul deliberately deviated from God's instructions (15:8-9), and "turned back from following" the LORD.

"It grieved Samuel; and he cried unto the LORD all night" (v. 11).

> "And Samuel said, Hath the LORD *as great* delight in burnt offerings and sacrifices, as in obeying the voice of the LORD? Behold, to obey *is* better than sacrifice, *and* to hearken than the fat of rams. For rebellion *is as* the sin of witchcraft, and stubbornness *is as* iniquity and idolatry. Because thou hast rejected the word of the LORD, he hath also rejected thee from *being* king" (1 Sam. 15:22-23).

> "And Samuel came no more to see Saul until the day of his death: nevertheless Samuel mourned for Saul: and the LORD repented that he had made Saul king over Israel" (1 Sam. 15:35).

God asked Samuel to quit grieving for Saul. He was to take with him a heifer for the sacrifice, go to Bethlehem and anoint one of Jesse's sons to be king (1 Sam. 16:1-13). See chapter 27, *Seeing Christ Typified in David and Solomon, page 152.*

Samuel, as their prophet, priest, and judge, anointed both Saul and David. But as long a Samuel lived he continued his official duties.

> "And Samuel judged Israel all the days of his life. And he went from year to year in circuit to Bethel, and Gilgal, and Mizpeh, and judged Israel in all those places. And his return *was* to Ramah; for there *was* his house; and there he judged Israel; and there he built an altar unto the LORD" (1 Sam. 7:15-17).

The comparisons by which Samuel foreshadowed Christ are worthy of note:.

- Both were wholly dedicated to God (1 Sam. 1:11; John 17:19)
- Both were born by divine intervention (1:20; Luke 1:35)
- Both testified in their adolescent years (2:18; Luke 2:46)
- Both grew in favor with God and men (2:26; Luke 2:52)

- Both heard and spoke the word of God (3:11; John 17:8)
- Both were endowed with profitable words (3:19; Luke 4:22)
- Both were God-ordained prophets (3:20; Acts 3:23)
- Both were God-ordained priests (2:35; Heb. 5:6, 10; 7:11
- Both were God-ordained judges (7:15-17; John 5:22)
- Both were given to intercessory prayer (12:23; Mark 1:35)
- Both were highly respected leaders (16:4; John 7:46)
- Both spoke to Saul(s) after their death (28:15; Acts 9:5)

"And Samuel died; and all the Israelites were gathered together, and lamented him, and buried him in his house at Ramah" (1 Sam. 25:1).

27

SEEING CHRIST TYPIFIED IN
DAVID AND SOLOMON

Foreshadowing Christ in His First and Second Advents Respectively

I. DAVID TYPIFIED CHRIST IN HIS FIRST ADVENT

David was the youngest of eight sons in an ordinary family in the village of Bethlehem. His outstanding characteristics were sincere love for and a profound trust in God. In early youth he bravely demonstrated this trust by slaying both a lion and a bear in defense of his father's sheep. God chose him to replace King Saul. He knew that David's heart was firmly anchored in God.

The Prophet Samuel may not yet have known anything of David. But God informed him that He had found "a man after his own heart" (1 Sam. 13:14), and had chosen him to be captain over His people. Later the Lord told him, "Fill thine horn with oil, and go, I will send thee to Jesse the Beth-lehemite: for I have provided me a king among his sons" (16:1).

> "And Samuel said, How can I go? if Saul hear *it,* he will kill me. And the LORD said, Take an heifer with thee, and say, I am come to sacrifice to the LORD. And call Jesse to the sacrifice, and I will show thee what thou shalt do: and thou shalt anoint unto me *him* whom I name unto thee" (1 Sam. 16:2-3).

It was announced in Bethlehem that Samuel had come to sacrifice to the Lord, but the anointing was kept secret for safety's sake. Samuel sanctified Jesse and his sons and called them to the sacrifice—*all but David.* He was out in the field taking care of the sheep. Samuel looked on Eliab, and thought, "Surely this is the one."

But God said, "I have not chosen him."

Then Jesse called Abinadab, and God had not chosen him. He brought Shammah. Wrong again. He made seven sons pass before Samuel, but none of them had been chosen. Now what?

Samuel asked Jesse, "Are these all the sons you have?"

Jesse said, "This is all I have—except the youngest. He's out with the sheep."

Samuel said, "Fetch him. We will not sit down till he comes." Ceremonially sanctified or not—David was the one God had chosen.

> "Then Samuel took the horn of oil, and anointed him in the midst of his brethren: and the spirit of the LORD came upon David from that day forward" (1 Sam. 16:13).

David's promotion was not announced in the *Bethlehem Post.* It was not displayed on banners across the village streets. The neighbors were not informed. His brothers were not impressed.

"But the Spirit of the LORD departed from Saul, and an evil spirit from the LORD troubled him" (16:14). He requested music to numb the pain of his guilt. Someone recommended David. David came. It worked. Saul loved him and he became Saul's armor-bearer. But if Saul had known that God had chosen David to be king he would have killed him. Once he sensed that, he tried most desperately to kill him.

David and Goliath

David had "returned from Saul to feed his father's sheep." The three oldest sons of Jesse were serving in Saul's army, and Goliath was on the scene. Jesse sent David with some food supplies, and to see how his brothers fare. David was disappointed that the army of the living God was afraid of this uncircumcised Philistine. Eliab's reaction reveals his misconception of David.

> "Eliab's anger was kindled against David, and he said, Why camest thou down hither? and with whom hast thou left those few sheep in the wilderness? I know thy pride, and the naughtiness of thine heart; for thou art come down that thou mightest see the battle" (1 Sam. 17:28).

David's focus was on God. He could not stand by and see reproach brought upon God's holy name by Goliath. David said to Saul, "Let no man's heart fail because of him; thy servant will go and fight with this Philistine. The LORD that delivered me out of the paw of the lion, and out of the paw of the bear, he will deliver me out of the hand of this Philistine."

> "And when the Philistine looked about, and saw David, he disdained him: for he was *but* a youth, and ruddy, and of a fair countenance. And the Philistine said unto David, *Am* I a dog, that thou comest to me with staves? And the Philistine cursed David by his gods. And the Philistine said to David, Come to me, and I will give thy flesh unto the fowls of the air, and to the beasts of the field.
> "Then said David to the Philistine, Thou comest to me with a sword, and with a spear, and with a shield: but I come to thee in the name of the LORD of hosts, the God of the armies of Israel, whom thou hast defied. This day will the LORD deliver thee into mine hand; and I will smite thee, and take thine head from thee; and I will give the carcases of the host of the Philistines this day unto the fowls of the air, and to the wild beasts of the earth; that all the earth may know that there is a God in Israel. And all this assembly shall know that the LORD saveth not with sword and spear: for the battle *is* the LORD'S, and he will give you into our hands" (1 Sam. 17:42-47).

> "And David put his hand in his bag, and took thence a stone, and slang *it,* and smote the Philistine in his forehead, that the stone sunk into his forehead; and he fell upon his face to the earth. So David prevailed over the Philistine with a sling and

with a stone, and smote the Philistine, and slew him; but *there was* no sword in the hand of David" (1 Sam. 17:49-50).

Never were two warriors so unequally matched—both ways. Physically, it was a ten foot giant with massive armor, shield and spear, defying a stripling shepherd boy armed only with a sling and a few stones. Spiritually (the way David saw it), it was the Eternal God, **The Omnipotent,** THE GREAT ALMIGHTY ONE coming against the lifeless little gods of wood and stone, that could neither speak, nor hear, nor see, nor move. **David gave God the glory.**

David and King Saul

Saul took David that day, and would not let him go home to his father's house. He set David over the men of war, and he was accepted in the sight of all the people, and also in the sight of Saul's servants. 1 Samuel 18:2, 5. But when the women celebrated, ascribing thousands to Saul, and ten thousands to David, Saul was very angry. From that day forth he was suspicious of David, and sought by all conceivable means to kill him.

"And David behaved himself wisely in all his ways; and the LORD was with him" (1 Sam. 18:5, 14, 30). Wherefore when Saul saw that [David] behaved himself very wisely, he was afraid of him. . . . And Saul saw and knew that the LORD was with David, . . . and Saul became David's enemy continually" (18:15, 28, 29). He sent messengers to kill him, "and Saul sought him every day, but God delivered him not into his hand" (19:11; 23:8, 14). He pursued David with an army of three thousand chosen men. Twice Saul had fallen into the hands of David and his men (24:2-7; 26:7-12), but David firmly refused to let his men harm "the LORD'S anointed."

David Portrayed Christ

In all these struggles David exemplified and typified Christ in His First Advent. The following similarities add beauty to the story.

- Both were born in the humble village of Bethlehem (1 Sam. 17:12; Mt. 2:1).
- Both shepherded their father's flock (1 Sam. 17:15; John 17:12).
- Both were obedient sons, of lowly estate on earth (1 Sam. 17:17; Lu. 2:51).
- Both were misunderstood by their brothers (1 Sam. 17:28; John 7:5).
- Both were sorely mistreated by high officials (1 Sam.19:1; Mark 15:15).
- Both fled as refugees from a king who sought to slay them (1 Sam 21:10; Mt. 2:14).
- Both had many enemies and suffered many conflicts (1 Sam. 23:8; Luke 4:29).
- Both were men after God's own heart (1 Sam. 13:14; John 8:29).
- Both were anointed long before they reigned (1 Sam. 16:13; John 18:37).
- Both were assured of their throne in spite of opposition (1 Sam. 24:20; Rev. 19:16).
- Both were prophets (Acts 2:29-30; Dt. 18:18) and kings (2 Sam. 5:4-5; John 18:37).
- Both wept over Jerusalem (David going out, 2 Sam. 15:30; Jesus coming in, Luke 19:41).
- Both had the promise of a house from the Father (2 Sam. 7:11-16; John 14:2).

David Typifies a _Greater David_

Both the house and kingdom of David have been extended into an eternal dimension in and by the **Greater David.** The following passages were written more than three hundred years after David the son of Jesse had died. Obviously they speak prophetically of an **Eternal David.**

"But they shall serve the LORD their God, and **David their king**, whom I will raise up unto them" (Jer. 30:9).

"And I will set up one shepherd over them, and he shall feed them, _even_ **my servant David**; he shall feed them, and he shall be their shepherd. And I the LORD will be their God, and **my servant David** a prince among them; I the LORD have spoken it" (Ezek. 34:23-24).

"Afterward shall the children of Israel return, and seek the LORD their God, and **David their king**; and shall fear the LORD and his goodness in the latter days" (Hosea 3:5).

This is not an exhaustive study of the life of David. We are looking primarily at those struggles in his early life which seem to typify Christ in His First Advent.

The Bible gives a much better report of David than it does of Solomon. "David did *that which was* right in the eyes of the LORD, and turned not aside from any *thing* that he commanded him all the days of his life, save only in the matter of Uriah the Hittite" (1 Kings 15:5). However, David was a man of war. For him to build the temple would have marred the type. The temple was to be built **by a man of peace in a time of peace**.

David was not a sinless man. He fell grievously, repented deeply (Psalms 32 and 51), and the LORD forgave him (2 Sam. 12:13). But for typological reasons Solomon, instead of David, needed to build the temple.

II. SOLOMON'S REIGN OF PEACE

Solomon's reign of peace and glory seems to have been designed and planned to typify Christ in His Second Coming. When he began to reign he first cleaned house. He executed Joab who had offended David (1 Kings 2:5, 28-34), and Adonijah who had defied Solomon by usurping the throne of David (2:22-25).   Shimei, who had also offended David (2 Sam. 16:5-9), Solomon restricted and later executed (1 Ki. 2:8, 36, 41-46). And Abiathar the priest, who had been a friend to David but later participated in Adonijah's conspiracy to the throne (1 Ki. 1:7, 19, 25), he thrust out of the priesthood (2:26-27). Then Solomon reigned in peace with royal majesty and glory.

Notice the typological similarity with what Christ will do when He comes again.

> "As therefore the tares are gathered and burned in the fire; so shall it be in the end of this world. The Son of man shall send forth his angels, and they shall gather out of his kingdom all things that offend, and them which do iniquity; and shall cast them into a furnace of fire: there shall be wailing and gnashing of teeth. Then shall the righteous shine forth as the sun in the kingdom of their Father. Who hath ears to hear, let him hear" (Mt. 13:40-43).

> "And then shall that Wicked be revealed, whom the Lord shall consume with the spirit of his mouth, and shall destroy with the brightness of his coming" (2 Thess. 2:8).

Solomon's reign began as a Utopia. No other king ever had so much going for him when he began to reign. His father, the greatest of Israel's earthly kings, had laid up *with all his might* enormous stores of gold, silver, brass, iron, wood, precious stones and marble stones (1 Chron. 29:2). David had encouraged all the people to give. The people were enthusiastic and they offered willingly.

Moreover God Himself had planned, even before Solomon's birth, that his reign should be free from war. God told David, "Behold, a son shall be born to thee, who shall be **a man of rest** [compare Mt. 11:28]; and I will give him rest from all his enemies round about: for his name shall be Solomon [**peace**], and I will give **peace and quietness unto Israel in his days**" (1 Chron. 22:9). His reign of peace was guaranteed before he was born. Not one king or nation rose up against Israel during the forty year reign of Solomon— foreshadowing the reign of Christ (Isa. 9:7).

To Solomon God said, "Wisdom and knowledge is granted unto thee: and I will give thee riches and wealth and honour, such as none of the kings have had that have been before thee, neither shall there any after thee have the like" (2 Chron. 1:12). Heaven and earth poured out their blessings upon

Solomon. His name was better and his throne greater than that of David (1 Kings 1:37, 47).

Solomon loved the Lord (1 Kings 3:3), and he "was beloved of his God" (Neh. 13:26). His God-given wisdom and glory have not been matched by mortal man. Everything was superlative. "And Judah and Israel dwelt safely, every man under his vine and under his fig tree, from Dan even to Beersheba, all the days of Solomon" (1 Kings 4:25). It typified what Messianic prophecies predict, such as:

> "But in the last days it shall come to pass, that the mountain of the house of the Lord shall be established in the top of the mountains, and it shall be exalted above the hills; and people shall flow into it And many nations shall come, and say, Come, and let us go up to the mountain of the Lord, and to the house of the God of Jacob; and he will teach us of his ways, and we will walk in his paths: for the law shall go forth of Zion, and the word of the Lord from Jerusalem. And he shall judge among many people, and rebuke strong nations afar off; and they shall beat their swords into plowshares, and their spears into pruning hooks: nation shall not lift up sword against nation, neither shall they learn war any more. But they shall sit every man under his vine and under his fig tree; and none shall make them afraid: for the mouth of the Lord of hosts hath spoken it" (Micah 4:1-4).

Solomon's early responses seemed flawless. He made wise choices that God could bless (2 Chron. 1:7-12). He communicated well with the people, and they highly respected him (2 Chron. 6:1-11. His fervent prayer was significantly inclusive (6:12-42). "The fire came down from heaven, and consumed the burnt offering, and the sacrifices; and the glory of the LORD filled the house" (7:1).

People came from far and near to hear Solomon's wisdom, and to see his glory. They found both his wisdom and his glory to surpass what they had expected. He wrote a thousand and five songs and three thousand proverbs. Thus far he typified our marvelous, invincible, adorable Christ. But there the typology ends—and **the tragedy begins**.

Solomon made affinity with Pharaoh and married his daughter (1 Kings 3:1). He married "women of the Moabites, Ammonites, Edomites, Zidonians, *and* Hittites; of the nations *concerning* which the LORD said . . . Ye shall not go in to them, neither shall they come in unto you: *for* surely they will turn away your heart after their gods: Solomon clave unto these in love" (11:1-2). He gathered women as *collectors' items*.

> "And he had seven hundred wives, princesses, and three hundred concubines: and his wives turned away his heart. For it came to pass, when Solomon was old, *that* his wives turned away his heart after other gods: and his heart was not perfect with the LORD his God, as *was* the heart of David his father.
>
> "For Solomon went after Ashtoreth the goddess of the Zidonians, and after Milcom the abomination of the Ammonites. And Solomon did evil in the sight of the LORD, and went not fully after the LORD, as *did* David his father.
>
> "Then did Solomon build an high place for Chemosh, the abomination of Moab, in the hill that *is* before Jerusalem, and for Molech, the abomination of the children of Ammon. And likewise did he for all his strange wives, which burnt incense and sacrificed unto their gods.
>
> "And the Lord was angry with Solomon, because his heart was turned from the LORD God of Israel " (1 Kings 11:3- 9).

Marriage is a sacred institution designed of God *for one man and one woman*. To multiply wives for self-gratification or political power is an abomination to God and a curse to man. The Mosaic law said a king "shall not multiply horses to himself, . . . Neither shall he multiply wives to himself, that his heart turn not away: neither shall he greatly multiply silver and gold" (Dt. 17:16-17). Solomon multiplied all three beyond reason—and enjoyed none. Nor do we have any record of his repentance, like that of his father.

The genealogy of Jesus bypasses Solomon. He is truly **the Son of David** (Mt. 1:1; 12:23; 21:9, 15; 22:42; Mk. 12:35), but He is not a son of Solomon. Matthew traces the Solomonic line down to "Joseph the husband of Mary, of whom was born Jesus, who is called Christ" (Mt. 1:16). But Luke traces the ancestry of Mary through her father Heli (the *father-in-law* of Joseph) back forty generations to **Nathan,** the son of David (Luke 3:23-31), a **brother** to Solomon (2 Sam. 5:14). This also explains why Jeremiah could say of King Jehoiakim, that "no man of his seed shall prosper, sitting upon the throne of David, and ruling any more in Judah" (Jer. 22:30; 36:30).

The life of Solomon has a sad ending. We will let him close the story with his own testimony.

> "Therefore I hated life; because the work that is wrought under the sun *is* grievous unto me: for all *is* vanity and vexation of spirit. Yea, I hated all my labour which I had taken under the sun: because I should leave it unto the man that shall be after me" (Eccl. 2:17-18).

28

SEEING CHRIST TYPIFIED IN
ELIJAH AND ELISHA

Elijah typified Christ's First Advent; Elisha typified His Second Advent
Jesus spoke of both in explanation of His own ministry (Luke 4:24-27)

I. ELIJAH, SINGLE AND HOMELESS

The Prophet Elijah, like Jesus in the flesh (Mt. 8:20), had no home of his own. Elijah's ministry was primarily prophetical and corrective. Like Jesus in His earthly ministry, Elijah encountered bitter enemies among the ruling classes.

Elijah came suddenly upon the scene, with a message of judgment from God upon the wicked King Ahab. "As the LORD God of Israel liveth, before whom I stand, there shall not be dew nor rain these years, but according to my word" (1 Kings 17:1b). His message was brief, pointed, and powerful. Then, by divine guidance, he went into hiding for three years. [Like Jesus when they wanted to stone Him, "hid himself . . . and so passed by" unharmed (John 8:59; 12:36).] The LORD directed and miraculously provided for Elijah. God said,

> "Get thee hence, and turn thee eastward, and **hide** thyself by the brook Cherith, that *is* before Jordan. And it shall be, *that* thou shalt drink of the brook; and I have commanded the ravens to feed thee there.
>
> "So he went and did according unto the word of the LORD: for he went and dwelt by the brook Cherith, that *is* before Jordan.

And the ravens brought him bread and flesh in the morning, and bread and flesh in the evening; and he drank of the brook. And it came to pass after a while, that the brook dried up, because there had been no rain in the land.

"And the word of the LORD came unto him, saying, Arise, get thee to Zarephath, which *belongeth* to Zidon, and dwell there: behold, I have commanded a widow woman there to sustain thee. So he arose and went to Zarephath. And when he came to the gate of the city, behold, the widow woman *was* there gathering of sticks: and he called to her, and said, Fetch me, I pray thee, a little water in a vessel, that I may drink.

"And as she was going to fetch *it,* he called to her, and said, Bring me, I pray thee, a morsel of bread in thine hand. And she said, *As* the LORD thy God liveth, I have not a cake, but an handful of meal in a barrel, and a little oil in a cruse: and, behold, I *am* gathering two sticks, that I may go in and dress it for me and my son, that we may eat it, and die.

"And Elijah said unto her, Fear not; go *and* do as thou hast said: but make me thereof a little cake first, and bring *it* unto me, and after make for thee and for thy son. For thus saith the LORD God of Israel, The barrel of meal shall not waste, neither shall the cruse of oil fail, until the day *that* the LORD sendeth rain upon the earth.

"And she went and did according to the saying of Elijah: and she, and he, and her house, did eat *many* days. *And* the barrel of meal wasted not, neither did the cruse of oil fail, according to the word of the LORD, which he spake by Elijah" (1 Ki. 17:3-16).

In the meantime the widow's son fell sick and died. Elijah "cried unto the LORD, and said, O LORD my God, I pray thee, let this child's soul come into him again. And the LORD heard the voice of Elijah; and the soul of the child came into him again, and he revived" (17:21-22).

"And the woman said to Elijah, Now by this I know that thou *art* a man of God, *and* that the word of the LORD in thy mouth *is* truth" (v. 24). [Jesus also did many miracles by which multitudes believed on Him (John 2:23; 4:39-42; 11:45; 12:42).]

After three and a half years (Luke 4:25) with neither rain nor dew, the famine in Samaria (the Northern Kingdom) was indeed very severe. Ahab blamed Elijah for it, but he could not harm him because he could not find him (1 Ki. 18:10).

Finally God told Elijah, "Go show thyself to Ahab; and I will send rain upon the earth."

> "And it came to pass, when Ahab saw Elijah, that Ahab said unto him, *Art* thou he that troubleth Israel? And he answered, I have not troubled Israel; but thou, and thy father's house, in that ye have forsaken the commandments of the LORD, and thou hast followed Baalim.
>
> "Now therefore send, and gather to me all Israel unto mount Carmel, and the prophets of Baal four hundred and fifty, and the prophets of the groves four hundred, which eat at Jezebel's table. So Ahab sent unto all the children of Israel, and gathered the prophets together unto mount Carmel. And Elijah came unto all the people, and said, How long halt ye between two opinions? if the LORD be God, follow him: but if Baal, then follow him. And the people answered him not a word" (1 Ki. 18:17-21).

Victory on Mount Carmel

The prophets of Baal were four hundred and fifty. Elijah said they should slay their bullock first. Twice he warned them to "put no fire under," but to call upon Baal to send fire. They "called on the name of Baal from morning even until noon, saying, O Baal, hear us. . . . And they cried aloud, and cut themselves . . . till the blood gushed out upon them. . . . And they prophesied until the time of the offering of the evening sacrifice," but Baal answered neither by voice nor fire.

Then Elijah prepared his bullock, "and put no fire under." As double proof, he dug a trench around his altar, and soaked his sacrifice with twelve barrels of water. Elijah prayed, "LORD God of Abraham, Isaac, and Israel, let it be known this day that thou art God in Israel, . . . Hear me, O LORD, hear me, that this people may know that thou art the LORD God, and that thou hast turned their heart back again" (1 Ki. 18:36-37).

"Then the fire of the LORD fell, and consumed the burnt sacrifice, and the wood, and the stones, and the dust, and licked up the water that *was* in the trench. And when all the people saw *it,* they fell on their faces: and they said, **The LORD, he *is* the God; the LORD, he *is* the God.** And Elijah said unto them, Take the prophets of Baal; let not one of them escape. And they took them: and Elijah brought them down to the brook Kishon, and slew them there" (18:38-40).

Elijah was sure, before there was any visible evidence, that the LORD would hear and answer his prayer (18:36-37, 41-46).   Jesus likewise, at the tomb of Lazarus, before Lazarus showed any signs of life, said,

"Father, I thank thee that thou hast heard me. And I knew that thou hearest me always: but because of the people which stand by I said it, that they may believe that thou hast sent me" (John 11:41-42).

Samaria acknowledged the LORD, and the drought was ended. In answer to Elijah's prayer, the LORD sent a great rain. "And Ahab rode, and went to Jezreel. And the hand of the LORD was on Elijah; and he girded up his loins, and ran before Ahab to the entrance of Jezreel" (1 Ki.18:46).

His Wilderness Temptation, and a Forty Day Fast

When Jezebel heard what Elijah had done, she sent him a message, binding herself with an oath, to slay him before the end of another day. Elijah fled for his life to Beersheba, which belongs to Judah (the Southern Kingdom), and left his servant there. But he himself went a day's journey into the wilderness, sat under a juniper tree, and requested that he might die (19:1-4).

From his mountain top experience he plunged into a valley of despair. That night, as Elijah slept, he was awakened twice by an angel of the LORD, who said, "Arise and eat." Each time food and water were providentially provided for him. And he "went in the strength of that meat forty days and forty nights unto Horeb the mount of God," into a cave and lodged there.

Rejuvenation on Mount Horeb

The LORD gave him a threefold demonstration of His *power*: a mighty wind that broke the rocks in pieces; an earthquake; and a fire. Then He manifested His *presence* and revealed His will with a still small voice, saying, "What doest thou here, Elijah?"

> Elijah said, "I have been very jealous for the LORD God of hosts: because the children of Israel have forsaken thy covenant, thrown down thine altars, and slain thy prophets with the sword; and I, *even* I only, am left; and they seek my life, to take it away" (1 Ki. 19:14).

The LORD sent Elijah back to Samaria. He commissioned him to anoint Hazael to be king over Syria; Jehu to be king over Israel; and Elisha to be prophet in Elijah's stead. Those first two were risky assignments, with the former kings still on the throne. But in the strength of the LORD he completed his work without flinching.

He confronted King Ahab face to face in the vineyard of Naboth.

> "Hast thou killed, and also taken possession? Thus saith the LORD, In the place where dogs licked the blood of Naboth shall dogs lick thy blood, even thine. . . . Behold, I will bring evil upon thee, and will take away thy posterity, . . . Him that dieth of Ahab in the city the dogs shall eat; and him that dieth in the field shall the fowls of the air eat "(1 Ki. 21:19-24).

When Ahab heard those words he humbled himself sincerely. And the LORD said to Elijah,

> "Because [Ahab] humbleth himself before me, I will not bring the evil in his days: but in his son's days I will bring the evil upon his house" (21:27-29).

Elijah in his struggles, homeless wanderings, absolute assurance in prayer, forty day fast, and then in his ascension to heaven, symbolized Christ in His First Advent.

II. ELISHA COMPLETES WHAT ELIJAH BEGAN

Elisha first appears when Elijah comes to anoint him. He must have been a well-to-do farmer. Elijah found him "plowing with twelve yoke of oxen before him, and he with the twelfth: and Elijah passed by him, and cast his mantle upon him" (1 Ki. 19:19).

> Elisha "left the oxen, and ran after Elijah, and said, Let me, I pray thee, kiss my father and my mother, and *then* I will follow thee. And he said unto him, Go back again: for what have I done to thee" (v. 20)?

I prefer Luther's German rendering: "Go back [home], and come again; consider what I have done to you." He gave him permission to *go back to his father, and come again*—typifying Jesus who has gone *back to His Father* and will *come again*. By asking, "What have I done to thee," Elijah surely intended Elisha to *consider the meaning* of casting his mantle upon him.

Elisha responded instantly, whole-heartedly, and with all seriousness.

> "And he returned back from him, and took a yoke of oxen, and slew them, and boiled their flesh with the instruments of the oxen, and gave unto the people, and they did eat. Then he arose, and went after Elijah, and ministered unto him" (v. 21).

The day of Elijah's departure (2 Kings 2) was an interesting day. All the prophets seemed to know that Elijah would be taken away that day. Three times Elijah said to Elisha, "Tarry here, I pray thee; for the LORD hath sent me to . . ." (from Gilgal to Bethel, from Bethel back to Jericho, and from Jericho to the Jordan). Each time Elisha said, "As the LORD liveth, and as thy soul liveth, I will not leave thee." Elisha proved to be firmly committed to his assignment.

At Bethel and at Jericho the prophets asked Elisha, "Knowest thou that the LORD will take away thy master from thy head today?" And he said, "Yea, I know it; hold ye your peace."

"And fifty men of the sons of the prophets went, and stood to view afar off: and they two stood by Jordan. And Elijah took his mantle, and wrapped *it* together, and smote the waters, and they were divided hither and thither, so that they two went over on dry ground.

"And it came to pass, when they were gone over, that Elijah said unto Elisha, Ask what I shall do for thee, before I be taken away from thee. And Elisha said, I pray thee, let a double portion of thy spirit be upon me. And he said, Thou hast asked a hard thing: *nevertheless,* if thou see me *when I am* taken from thee, it shall be so unto thee; but if not, it shall not be *so.*

"And it came to pass, as they still went on, and talked, that, behold, *there appeared* a chariot of fire, and horses of fire, and parted them both asunder; and Elijah went up by a whirlwind into heaven. And Elisha saw *it,* and he cried, My father, my father, the chariot of Israel, and the horsemen thereof. And he saw him no more: and he took hold of his own clothes, and rent them in two pieces" (2 Ki. 2:7-12).

Elisha took up the mantle that fell from Elijah, and very solemnly returned to the River Jordan. Minutes before the two had crossed that river together (the river that often symbolizes the victorious death of saints—this time, the death of Christ, followed by ascension). Like Eleazar descending from Mount Hor, wearing the high priestly garments in which Aaron had ascended (See chapter twenty-three), even so Elisha carried the mantle that fell from Elijah. His return prefigures the return of Christ.

In his musings Elisha remembered their last recorded words before Elijah rose out of his sight. "Ask what I shall do for thee, before I be taken away from thee," Elijah had offered.

Elisha requested, "Let a double portion of thy spirit be upon me."

"If thou see me when I am taken from thee, it shall be so unto thee," said Elijah.

Elisha did see him go. His request was granted.

"And he took the mantle of Elijah that fell from him, and smote the waters, and said, Where *is* the LORD God of Elijah? and when he also had smitten the waters, they parted hither and thither: and Elisha went over.

"And when the sons of the prophets which *were* to view at Jericho saw him, they said, The spirit of Elijah doth rest on Elisha. And they came to meet him, and **bowed themselves to the ground before him**" (2 Ki. 2:14-15).

We have record of only one man falling on his knees before Elijah (2 Ki. 1:13). When Jesus comes again, "every knee shall bow, of things in heaven, and things in earth, and things under the earth; and every tongue shall confess that Jesus Christ is Lord, to the glory of God the Father" (Phil. 2:10-11).

After Elijah and Elisha crossed the River Jordan (a symbol of death), "Elijah went up by a whirlwind into heaven" (2 Ki. 2:11b). Elisha "took up also the mantle of Elijah that fell from him" (assuming the office of Elijah, with a double portion of Elijah's spirit) and returned (typifying the Second Coming of our resurrected, ascended, and returning Savior and Lord). When Jesus comes again no one will withstand Him. This was typified in the life and power of Elisha whom no one threatened or withstood in his peaceful and powerful ministry.

The Life of Elisha a Foreshadow of Christ

We need not look for a specific type of Jesus in every act of Elisha, and we realize that some of his works are equally typical of Jesus' First Advent. However, he was the direct successor of Elijah who had gone to heaven. He had received "a double portion of [Elijah's] spirit," and we have no indication that he was ever challenged by enemies. These unusual features are more typical of Christ in His Second Coming than in His First Advent. Some of the twenty miracles of Elisha foreshadowed Christ's life and work when He was here in the flesh. Others will be fulfilled in the Regeneration when He comes again!.

Twenty Signs Recorded in 2 Kings

1. Parted the waters of Jordan like Elijah had done (2:14)
2. The prophets bowed to the ground before him (2:15)
3. Waters at Jericho were healed through Elisha (2:19-22)
4. Without rain, ditches were filled with water (3:16-18)
5. Widow's oil was multiplied to pay her debt (4:1-7)
6. A barren couple at Shunem had a miracle child (4:16-17)
7. The child was restored to life after death (4:18-35)
8. Poisonous pottage was fully healed (4:38-41)
9. He fed a hundred men with 20 barley loaves (4:42-44)
10. Naaman was healed of leprosy (5:14)
11. Gahazi incurred the leprosy of Naaman (5:20-27)
12. Iron made to swim (6:1-7). The dead will rise when Jesus comes.
13. Gave divine counsel to the King of Israel (6:8-12)
14. Blinded the Syrian army, (6:13-21)
15. Foretold the coming of Joram's messenger (6:30-33)
16. Foretold of food aplenty tomorrow (7:1-18)
17. Foretold seven years of famine (8:1-6)
18. Foretold Benhadad's death and Hazael's brutality (8:7-15)
19. Foretold Joash's limited victories (13:14-19)
20. Dead man revived upon touching Elisha's bones (13:21)

Of the above signs, the following (identified by numbers from the previous list) especially prefigured Christ.

Types of Christ's Second Advent

(1) Coming back after crossing the Jordan (type of death), typifies Jesus coming again.
(2) Every knee will bow to Jesus when He comes (Phil. 2:10).
(3) Jesus was and still is "the Lord that healeth thee" (Ex. 15:26; Rev. 22:2)

(4) Jesus was and will be the water of life to every Christian (John 7:37; Rev. 22:1)

(7) Jesus is the Resurrection and the Life (John 11:25)

(10) Jesus healed and still heals our spiritual leprosy (Acts 4:12)

(12) The "stick" that was cut (2 Ki. 6:6) typifies Jesus "cut off out of the land of the living" (Isa. 53:8); and the iron rising from the bottom of the Jordan typifies the resurrection from the dead when Jesus comes again. (1 Thess. 4:16; Phil. 3:11).

(14) "In that day I will . . . smite every horse of the people [or nations] with blindness" (Zech. 12:4)

(20) Only Jesus and the bones of Elisha have affected resurrection by their own death.

Elijah and Elisha had each restored a corpse to life, but touching the bones of Elisha had restored one man after Elisha's death. Christ, by His death, has already, and will yet restore countless multitudes to life.

Part IV

Seeing Christ
in
Eternity Future

"Unto him be glory . . . throughout all ages, world without end. Amen"

Eph. 3:21

29

SEEING CHRIST,
THE REAL HEBREW SERVANT

Committed "for ever"

"Now these are the judgments which thou shalt set before them. If thou buy an Hebrew servant, six years he shall serve: and in the seventh he shall go out free for nothing. If he came in by himself, he shall go out by himself: if he were married, then his wife shall go out with him. If his master have given him a wife, and she have born him sons or daughters; the wife and her children shall be her master's, and he shall go out by himself. And if the servant shall plainly say, I love my master, my wife, and my children; I will not go out free: Then his master shall bring him unto the judges; he shall also bring him to the door, or unto the door post; and his master shall bore his ear through with an awl; and he shall serve him for ever" (Ex. 21:1-6).

I often wondered, Why should the master pierce the ear of a bond servant who thus declares his love and loyalty, **first** for his master, **then** for his own wife and children? A friend explained that it typifies Christ's commitment, **first** and above all to God, **then** to His church. Immediately I appreciated his analysis, but at first thought I had one problem. How could Jesus, who was perfectly one with His Father (John 14:8-11), be a *bond servant* "for ever"?

On second thought I recalled that Jesus, "who, **being in the form of God**, thought it not robbery to be equal with God: but made himself of no reputation, and [voluntarily] **took**

upon him the form of a servant, . . . he humbled himself, and became obedient unto death, even the death of the cross" (Phil. 2:6-8). That solved my problem.

There we have both facts plainly stated in New Testament doctrine. Each time the word form is translated from *morphe* (# 3444) in Greek. It is the central part of our English *metamorphosis* (the process which transforms a caterpillar into a butterfly). *Morphe* is found only three times in the Bible (Mark 16:12; Phil. 2:6, 7), and is used only of Jesus Incarnate. From eternity past He had been in the form (*morphe*) of God, but in His incarnation He voluntarily took upon Him the *form* of a slave, deliberately condescending to the role of a bond servant. Isaiah had foretold the fulfillment of that commitment seven hundred years in advance.

> "The Lord GOD hath **opened mine ear** [*as with an awl*], and I was not rebellious, neither turned away back. I gave my back to the smiters, and my cheeks to them that plucked off the hair: I hid not my face from shame and spitting" (Isa 50:5-6).

The Psalmist likewise quotes Jesus as saying, "Sacrifice and offering thou didst not desire; **mine ears hast thou opened** [*in keeping with Ex. 21:6*]: burnt offering and sin offering hast thou not required. Then said I, Lo, I come: in the volume of the book *it is* written of me, **I delight to do thy will, O my God:** yea, thy law *is* within my heart" (Ps. 40:6-8).

Both passages correspond with those from Exodus and Philippians above. Jesus did not turn back from cruel torture, nor did He hide His face from shame and spitting. He submitted willingly, even unto crucifixion, like the execution of a criminal slave. He made that commitment and never deviated from it.

> "For I came down from heaven, not to do mine own will, but the will of him that sent me" (John 6:38)

> "For whether is greater, he that sitteth at meat, or he that serveth? is not he that sitteth at meat? but I am among you as he that serveth" (Luke 22:27).

In the Tabernacle furniture wood is considered as typifying the humanity of Christ. The piercing of a servant's ear was done at a [*wooden*] door or post, the place where the blood of the Passover lamb was applied (Ex. 12:7). Jesus gave His life on a *wooden* cross. The law could not demand it, for He had fully met every requirement of the law. Legally He could have *gone out by himself, free for nothing.* Was not that the agonizing cry of His flesh in Gethsemane?

> And he went forward a little, and fell on the ground, and prayed that, if it were possible, the hour might pass from him. And he said, Abba, Father, all things *are* possible unto thee; take away this cup from me: nevertheless not what I will, but what thou wilt" (Mark 14:35-36).

> "And being in an agony he prayed more earnestly: and his sweat was as it were great drops of blood falling down to the ground" (Luke 22:44).

> "The spirit indeed is willing, but the flesh is weak" (Mark 14:38b).

Did Jesus say that solely of His disciples? Was He not also disclosing the struggle of His own flesh? He "was in all points tempted like as we are, yet without sin" (Heb. 4:15b).

> "Now My soul is troubled, and what shall I say? 'Father, save Me from this hour'? But for this purpose I came to this hour" (John 12:27, NKJ).

> "Then said Jesus unto them, When ye have lifted up the Son of man, then shall ye know that I am *he,* and *that* I do nothing of myself; but as my Father hath taught me, I speak these things. And he that sent me is with me: the Father hath not left me alone; for I do always those things that please him" (John 8:28-29).

When mortal bond servants committed themselves to serve their master "for ever," there was after all a time limit set by the brevity of life. Not so with Jesus! His resurrection provides an eternal dimension to His commitment. That was not literally true of any other **Hebrew servant.**

Our text from Exodus speaks of the master having given the servant a wife. Jesus abundantly proved His love, first for

His *Master*, then for His *bride and children* whom the Father gave Him.

> "All that the Father giveth me shall come to me; and him that cometh to me I will in no wise cast out" (John 6:37).

> "I have manifested thy name unto the men which thou gavest me out of the world: thine they were, and thou gavest them me; and they have kept thy word. . . . I pray for them: I pray not for the world, but for them which thou hast given me; for they are thine. And all mine are thine, and thine are mine; and I am glorified in them. . . . those that thou gavest me I have kept, . . . " (John 17:6, 9-10, 12b).

> **". . . having loved his own which were in the world, he loved them unto the end" (John 13:1b).**

No mortal servant ever loved his master, or his wife and children, like Jesus loved those whom His Father gave Him. Nor has any mortal servant ever served his master as faithfully as Jesus serves the Father who sent Him. All others are only a shadow of which Jesus is the Substance.

Jesus refused to go out by Himself, free, because He loved His Master (the Father). ". . .Christ also loved the church, and gave himself for it; That he might sanctify and cleanse it with the washing of water by the word, That he might present it to himself a glorious church, not having spot, or wrinkle, or any such thing; but that it should be holy and without blemish"(Eph 5:25-27).

Christ is the **True Hebrew Servant**, *committed to serve the Father for ever.* Ever since His ascension to Glory His intercessory ministry never ceased. Even when He reigns as King of Kings and LORD of Lords— yea, in **Eternity Future** He will be serving His Father "**for ever.**"

30
SEEING CHRIST,
THE FOURFOLD MESSIANIC BRANCH

I. THE ROYAL BRANCH

"Jesus answered , Thou sayest that I am a king.
To this end was I born, . . ." (John 18:37).

"And there shall come forth a rod out of the stem of Jesse, and a **Branch** shall grow out of his roots: And the spirit of the LORD shall rest upon him, the spirit of wisdom and understanding, the spirit of counsel and might, the spirit of knowledge and of the fear of the LORD; And shall make him of quick understanding in the fear of the LORD: and he shall not judge after the sight of his eyes, neither reprove after the hearing of his ears: But with righteousness shall he judge the poor, and reprove with equity for the meek of the earth: and he shall smite the earth with the rod of his mouth, and with the breath of his lips shall he slay the wicked. And righteousness shall be the girdle of his loins, and faithfulness the girdle of his reins" (Isa 11:1-5).

Isaiah reconfirmed the promise God had made to David more than two hundred years earlier. "And thine house and thy kingdom shall be established for ever before thee: thy throne shall be established for ever" (2 Sam. 7:16). "The stem of Jesse" identifies the Davidic dynasty, and thereby the royalty of the **Branch**, the unique Son of David. That promise can be fulfilled in none other than our Lord Jesus Christ, the ROYAL BRANCH of whom Isaiah spoke. On Him rest the seven Spirits of God. No other kingdom will endure for ever.

The royalty of Christ is unique. He is not only the Son of David, but the Son of God as well. The Davidic dynasty is unique. David's name is frequently attached to Christ. Thirteen times in the Synoptic Gospels Jesus is identified as **the Son of David** (Mt. 9:27; 12:23; 15:22; 20:30, 31; 21:9, 15; 22:42; Mark 10:47, 48; 12:35; Luke 18:38, 39). And the name *David* is used for Christ Himself at least four times in Messianic prophecies, written more than three hundred years after King David had died (Jer. 30:9; Ezek. 34:23, 24; Hosea 3:5). Christ is the **Greater David.**

"And in that day there shall be a **root of Jesse**, which shall stand for an ensign of the people; to it shall the Gentiles seek: and his rest shall be glorious. And it shall come to pass in that day, *that* the Lord shall set his hand again the second time to recover the remnant of his people, which shall be left, from Assyria, and from Egypt, and from Pathros, and from Cush, and from Elam, and from Shinar, and from Hamath, and from the islands of the sea. And he shall set up an ensign for the nations, and shall assemble the outcasts of Israel, and gather together the dispersed of Judah from the four corners of the earth" (Isa. 11:10-12).

Christ is a "**root** of Jesse" as well as "a **Branch** that shall grow out of his roots" (11:2). Normally the root bears the tree while the tree bears the branches. But spiritually, Christ is **the Root and the Branch** that bears up, and enhances with special meaning His entire *ancestral tree.*

********   ********   ********

II. THE RIGHTEOUS BRANCH
"The LORD Our Righteousness" (Jer. 23:6).

"Behold, the days come, saith the LORD, that I will raise unto David a righteous Branch, and a King shall reign and prosper, and shall execute judgment and justice in the earth. In his days Judah shall be saved, and Israel shall dwell safely: and this is his name whereby he shall be called, THE LORD OUR RIGHTEOUSNESS" (Jer 23:5-6).

"Behold, the days come, saith the LORD, that I will perform that good thing which I have promised unto the house of Israel and to the house of Judah. In those days, and at that time, will I cause the **Branch of righteousness** to grow up unto David; and he shall execute judgment and righteousness in the land. In those days shall Judah be saved, and Jerusalem shall dwell safely: and this *is the name* wherewith she shall be called, The LORD **our righteousness**" (Jer 33:14-16).

In both passages *Branch* is capitalized. Both speak of His royalty, but their main emphasis is on His righteousness. He is "THE LORD [Jehovah] OUR RIGHTEOUSNESS" (23:6b). As for man, "There is none righteous, no, not one"(Rom.3:10). "We are all as an unclean thing, and all our **righteousnesses** [plural] are as filthy rags" (Isa. 64:6). Therefore we are totally dependent upon **His righteousness** [singular] for our salvation.

That truth of the gospel is what unbelievers fail to recognize. "For they being ignorant of God's righteousness, and going about to establish their own righteousness, have not submitted themselves unto the righteousness of God"(Rom 10:3). Luther's German translation says they are not obedient to the **righteousness that counts with God.** Our righteousness is tainted with sin, contaminated, and far too anemic to count with God!

The righteousness of Christ is doubly unique. First, He lived in the flesh for thirty-three years, "was in all points tempted like as we are, yet without sin" (Heb. 4:15). He *did no sin, knew no sin, and in him was no sin* (2 Cor. 5:21; 1 Pet. 2:22; 1 John 3:5). He is righteousness personified, yet He willingly died on the cross to atone for our sins! *Second*, His is the only righteousness that can be transmitted to another, and that only to believers who trust in His blood for their salvation.

"By faith Noah . . . became heir of the righteousness which is by faith" (Heb. 11:7). Abraham "believed in the LORD," and the Lord counted his faith "for righteousness"(Gen. 15:6; Rom. 4:3). The righteousness of Christ was credited to their account because they believed God's promise of a coming Savior.

Christ is the One "whom God hath set forth *to be* a propitiation through faith in his blood, to declare his righteousness for the remission of sins that are past, through the forbearance of God; To declare, *I say*, at this time his righteousness: that he might be just, and the justifier of him which believeth in Jesus"(Rom 3:25-26). **The righteousness of Christ is the only way to heaven!**

********   ********   ********

III. THE SERVANT BRANCH
"I am among you as He that serveth" (Luke 22:27).

"Behold, I will bring forth **my servant the BRANCH.** For behold the stone that I have laid before Joshua; upon one stone shall be seven eyes: behold, I will engrave the graving thereof, saith the LORD of hosts, and I will remove the iniquity of that land in one day. In that day, saith the LORD of hosts, shall ye call every man his neighbour under the vine and under the fig tree" (Zech. 3:8b-10).

Branch, in the Jeremiah and Zechariah passages, is translated from the Hebrew *tsemach* (# 6780), meaning sprout. It prefigured the lowly birth of Christ Incarnate, springing forth from the Davidic line and far surpassing all human ancestry or royalty.

"Who, being in the form of God, thought it not robbery to be equal with God: But made himself of no reputation, and took upon him **the form of a servant**, and was made in the likeness of men: And being found in fashion as a man, he humbled himself, and became obedient unto death, even the death of the cross" (Phil 2:6-8).

"Even as the Son of man came not to be ministered unto, but to minister, and to give his life a ransom for many" (Mt. 20:28). "I am among you as one that serveth" (Lu. 22:27b).

These verses all speak of His Royal Servanthood. He came to render a service to man that no other being could possibly have accomplished. Although His deity remained unchallenged and His royalty exceeds all others, enroute to the throne He willingly embraced the Cross—to die for us!

"Behold the man whose name *is* **The BRANCH**; and he shall grow up out of his place, and he shall build the temple of the LORD: Even he shall build the temple of the LORD; and he shall bear the glory, and shall sit and rule upon his throne; and **he shall be a priest upon his throne**: and the counsel of peace shall be between them both" (Zech. 6:12b-13).

The crowns placed upon Joshua the priest, did not make him king (6:11-13). It was only a symbolic coronation prefiguring Christ as both King and Priest. Those crowns were then kept "for a memorial in the temple" (v. 14). Other than this brief coronation only Melchizedek typified Christ as both King and Priest. Others suffered dire consequences seeking to combine those two offices. King Saul lost his kingdom (1 Sam. 13:11-14) and King Uzziah became leprous for life (2 Chron. 26:16-21). The Royal Priesthood of Christ spiraled to a climax at Calvary and continues with His intercessory ministry ever since. Both are integral aspects of **His Royal Servanthood.**

********   ********   ********

IV. THE MOST HIGH BRANCH

"Thus saith the Lord GOD [Adonai Jehovah]; I will also take the **highest branch** of the high cedar, and will set it; I will crop off from the top of his young twigs a **tender one**, and will plant it upon a high mountain [*probably Mount Zion*] and eminent" (Ezek. 17:22).

The *highest branch*, in this case uncapitalized, apparently refers to the royal lineage of David, the highest, most eminent dynasty of "the high Cedar" [undivided Israel]. Christ, in His lowly birth, was indeed a *tender one*, cropped off from the very top of Israel's young twigs. He came to earth as a tiny twig, but has certainly surpassed all others! Look what the Lord GOD [Adonai Jehovah] is doing with that Select Twig. He already is, and for ever will be, **The Most High Branch.**

"In the mountain of the height of Israel I will plant it [*the tender One*]: and it shall bring forth boughs, and bear fruit, and be a goodly cedar: and under it shall dwell all fowl of every wing; in the shadow of the branches thereof shall they dwell. And all the trees of the field [*every nation on earth*] shall know that I the LORD [Jehovah] have brought down the high tree, have exalted the low tree, have dried up the green tree, and have made the dry tree to flourish: I the LORD have spoken and have done it" (Ezek. 17:23-24).

"For unto us a child is born [*the tender One*], unto us a son is given: and the government shall be upon his shoulder: and his name shall be called Wonderful, Counsellor, The mighty God, The everlasting Father, The Prince of Peace. Of the increase of *his* government and peace *there shall be* no end, upon the throne of David, and upon his kingdom, to order it, and to establish it with judgment and with justice from henceforth even for ever. The zeal of the LORD of hosts will perform this" (Isa. 9:6-7).

"I saw in the night visions, and, behold, *one* like the Son of man came with the clouds of heaven, and came to the Ancient of days, and they brought him near before him. And there was given him dominion, and glory, and a kingdom, that all people, nations, and languages, should serve him: his dominion *is* an everlasting dominion, which shall not pass away, and his kingdom *that* which shall not be destroyed" (Dan 7:13-14).

"Wherefore God also hath highly exalted him, and given him a name which is above every name: That at the name of Jesus every knee should bow, of *things* in heaven, and *things* in earth, and *things* under the earth; And *that* every tongue should confess that Jesus Christ *is* Lord, to the glory of God the Father" (Phil. 2:9-11).

"And he hath on *his* vesture and on his thigh a name written, KING OF KINGS, AND LORD OF LORDS" (Rev.19:16).

Eternity Future will prove Christ to be superlative in **Royalty, Inherent Righteousness, Faithful Servanthood,** and in perfect , inseperable **Union with the MOST HIGH GOD**. "For in Him dwelleth all the fulness of the Godhead bodily" (Col. 2:9).

ABBREVIATIONS

Old Testament Books		New Testament Books	
Gen.	Genesis	Mt.	Matthew
Ex.	Exodus	Mk.	Mark
Lev.	Leviticus	Lu.	Luke
Nu.	Numbers	Jn.	John
Dt.	Deuteronomy	Acts	Acts
Josh.	Joshua	Rom.	Romans
Judg.	Judges	1 Cor.	1 Corinthians
Ruth	Ruth	2 Cor.	2 Corinthians
1 Sam.	1 Samuel	Gal.	Galatians
2 Sam.	2 Samuel	Eph.	Ephesians
1 Ki.	1 Kings	Phil.	Philippians
2 Ki.	2 Kings	Col.	Colossians
1 Chron.	1 Chronicles	1 Thes.	1 Thessalonians
2 Chron.	2 Chronicles	2 Thes.	2 Thessalonians
Ezra	Ezra	1 Tim.	1 Timothy
Neh.	Nehemiah	2 Tim.	2 Timothy
Esth.	Esther	Titus	Titus
Job	Job	Philem.	Philemon
Ps.	Psalms	Heb.	Hebrews
Prov.	Proverbs	Jas.	James
Eccl.	Ecclesiastes	1 Pet.	1 Peter
S. of S.	Song of Solomon	2 Pet.	2 Peter
Isa.	Isaiah	1 Jn.	1 John
Jer.	Jeremiah	2 Jn.	2 John
Lam.	Lamentations	3 Jn.	3 John
Ezek.	Exekiel	Jude	Jude
Dan.	Daniel	Rev.	Revelation
Hos.	Hosea		
Joel	Joel		
Amos	Amos		
Obad.	Obadiah		
Jonah	Jonah		
Mic.	Micah		
Nah.	Nahum		
Hab.	Habakkuk		
Zeph.	Zephaniah		
Hag.	Haggai		
Zech.	Zechariah		
Mal.	Malachi		

BIBLIOGRAPHY

Davidson, Professor F. ed. *The New Bible Commentary.* Grand Rapids, MI: WM. B. Eerdmans Publishing Company, 1963.

Douglas, J. D. ed. *The New Bible Dictionary.* Grand Rapids, MI: WM. B. Eerdmans Publishing Company,

Habershon, Ada R. *The Study of the Types.* Grand Rapids, MI: Kregel Publications, 1974.

Lockyer, Herbert. *All the Men of the Bible.* Grand Rapids, MI: Zondervan Publishing House, 1958.

Pink, Arthur W. *Gleanings in Genesis.* Chicago: Moody Press, Copyright by The Moody Bible Institute, 1922.

Pink, Arthur W. *Gleanings in Exodus.* Chicago: Moody Press, No copyright indicated.

Stone, Nathan. *Names of God.* Chicago: The Moody Bible Institute, 1944.

Strong, James. *Strong's Exhaustive Concordance of the Bible.* New York: Abingdon-Cokesbury Press, 1951.

Tenney, Merril C. ed. Zondervan Pictorial Bible Dictionary. Grand Rapids, MI: Zondervan Publishing House, 1963.

Wood. Nathan R. *The Trinity in the Universe.* Grand Rapids, MI: Kregel Publications, 1984.

Young, Robert. *Young's Analytical Concordance.* Grand Rapids, Michigan: Associated Publishers.

Although I used very few quotes (none without permission and proper acknowledgment), these books were used in my research and study. I am especially indebted to Strong's and Young's Concordances, and *Names of God* by Nathan Stone, for their help with Hebrew names for God.   Without their help and confirmation this book would not be written.